REDUCING
SCHOOL

VIOLENCE

THROUGH
CONFLICT
RESOLUTION

DAVID W. JOHNSON • ROGER T. JOHNSON

ASSOCIATION FOR SUPERVISION AND CURRICULUM DEVELOPMENT

ALEXANDRIA, VIRGINIA

Association for Supervision and Curriculum Development
1250 N. Pitt Street, Alexandria, Virginia 22314
Telephone: 703-549-9110, Fax: 703-549-3891

ASCD publications present a variety of viewpoints. The views expressed or implied in this book should not be interpreted as official positions of the Association.

Printed in the United States of America.

Ronald S. Brandt, *Director of Publications*
Nancy Modrak, *Managing Editor, ASCD Books*
Margaret A. Oosterman, *Associate Editor*
Tracey A. Smith, *Print Production Coordinator*
Gary Bloom, *Manager, Design and Production Services*
Valerie Sprague, *Desktop Publisher*

From the Editors: We welcome readers' comments on ASCD books and other publications. If you would like to give us your opinion of this book or suggest topics for future books, please write to ASCD, Managing Editor of Books, 1250 N. Pitt St., Alexandria, VA 22314.

About the Authors: David W. Johnson is Professor of Educational Psychology, and Roger T. Johnson is Professor of Curriculum and Instruction; both are codirectors of the Cooperative Learning Center, University of Minnesota, College of Education, 202 Pattee Hall, 150 Pillsbury Drive S.E., Minneapolis, MN 55455-0298; telephone: 612-624-7031.

ASCD Stock No.: 1-95198
ISBN 0-87120-252-2

Library of Congress Cataloging-in-Publication Data

Johnson, David W., 1940-
    Reducing school violence through conflict resolution / David W.
    Johnson and Roger T. Johnson.
        p.   cm.
    "ASCD Stock No.: 1-95198"—T.p. verso.
    Includes bibliographical references.
    ISBN 0-87120-252-2 (pbk.)
    1. School violence—United States—Prevention. 2. Conflict
    management—United States.   I. Johnson, Roger T., 1938- .
    II. Title.
    LB3013.3.J65 1995
    371.5'8—dc20   95-32482
                                                                CIP

Reducing School Violence
Through Conflict Resolution

Foreword

In the recently completed session, the Texas legislature enacted legislation mandating that the topic of conflict resolution be addressed in professional development activities across the state. Although one might question the validity of mandating a specific topic for such activities on school campuses, the action certainly reflects the current national interest in conflict resolution.

Do you address resolution of conflict within the context of win-lose? David and Roger Johnson, the authors of this practical and informative book, would chide us if we answered yes. They identify alternative strategies to the win-lose approach.

Increasing violence and threats of violence in U.S. schools have prompted many school districts to take aggressive action in providing greater security and more positive learning environments. Schools are spending significant amounts of money to address safety concerns. Can schools invest in strategies other than a police force, surveillance equipment, and metal detectors to manage violence and conflict? The authors present a strong case for using an alternative approach. By training students in conflict resolution, educators can help school environments become more orderly and peaceful while instruction is improving. Additionally, students gaining skills in their school years will be better in managing conflicts in future years.

Reducing School Violence Through Conflict Resolution identifies specific programs and activities to reduce violence and stresses that educators should follow a sequence of steps in implementing violence prevention and conflict resolution programs. School personnel should realize that there are no quick-fix solutions. The authors note that reducing violence is a long-term project: "It took 30 years to reduce smoking in the United States and 15 years to reduce drunk driving—reducing violence make take even longer." As schools implement conflict resolution/peer mediation training, the authors emphasize that student training should be repeated for 12 years, with increasing levels of complexity and sophistication.

Are you interested in better preparing students for the future? If you could provide specific training for students in an area that would result in their being more likely to gain career opportunities, obtain successful careers, build and maintain a lifelong set of friends and a cohesive and caring family, and generally enjoy a higher quality of life, would you strongly consider implementing such a program? The authors believe that conflict resolution/peer mediation training will bring these results.

Educators searching for ways to reduce violence in school settings will discover in this book practical and specific strategies for implementing violence prevention and conflict resolution programs. Classroom teachers desiring to make their classrooms more stimulating while providing an environment for students to manage conflicts of interest will find it especially helpful as a resource.

—CHARLES E. PATTERSON
ASCD President, 1995–96

Preface

Teaching students the procedures and skills they need to resolve conflicts constructively has been relatively ignored. Despite the large amount of time teachers and students spend in dealing with destructively managed conflicts, and despite considerable research evidence indicating that the constructive management of conflict increases classroom productivity, teachers receive little training in how to use conflict for instructional purposes and how to teach students conflict management. In essence, teachers have been implicitly taught to avoid and suppress conflicts and to fear conflicts when they burst forth—actions that make them worse.

This book is about teaching students to be peacemakers. It includes practical strategies as well as specific suggestions to teach conflict resolution procedures and skills. Such work requires training, perseverance, and support. Training is a good start to the process, but a year or two of classroom experience may be needed before the procedures and skills become a natural part of teaching. The results for students are well worth the effort.

We have spent nearly 30 years building the theory, research, and practical experience required to write this book. In the 1960s, we began by reviewing the research, conducting our initial research studies, and training teachers in the classroom use of constructive conflict. Since then our work has proliferated. Yet the concept of constructively managed conflict is older than our work. Our roots reach back to Morton Deutsch and Kurt Lewin.

Many teachers have taught us procedures for training students to be peacemakers and have field-tested our ideas in their classrooms with considerable success. We have been in their classrooms, and we have taught beside them. We appreciate their ideas and celebrate their successes. Talented and productive graduate students have conducted research studies that have made significant contributions to our understanding of conflict. We feel privileged to have worked with them.

1

Increasing Violence: A Concern for Schools

Teaching is different from what it used to be. Fifty years ago, the main disciplinary problems were running in halls, talking out of turn, and chewing gum. Today's transgressions include physical and verbal violence, incivility, and in some schools, drug abuse, robbery, assault, and murder. The result is that many teachers spend an inordinate amount of time and energy managing classroom conflicts (Amsler and Sadella 1987). When students poorly manage their conflicts with each other and with faculty, aggression results (McCormick 1988, Kreidler 1984). Such behavior is usually punished with detentions, suspensions, and expulsions (Ray, Kestner, and Freedman 1985).

As violence increases, pressure for safe and orderly schools increases. Schools are struggling with what to do. This book offers two interrelated approaches: a violence prevention program and a conflict resolution program. Examining violence in schools and society and the influences that support violence helps us understand why we need such programs.

Violence in Schools

The number of violence incidences in schools is increasing. The National League of Cities reports that between 1990 and 1994, 33 percent of member cities had a significant increase in school violence (a student killed or seriously injured), and in 1993–94, school violence increased 55 percent in large cities and 41 percent in cities of 100,000 or more. Ten percent of teachers and nearly one-fourth of students in public schools say that they have been the victim of a violent act in school (Hamburger 1993). In 1993, one-fourth of all high school seniors reported they had been threatened with violence ("Stop the Violence" 1994).

Although these statistics indicate that school violence is increasing, some studies suggest that the seriousness may be overstated. Opotow (1991) interviewed 40 inner-city 7th graders and found that about two-thirds described school conflicts as violent. In reality, the fights were usually infrequent scuffles that caused no or minor injury. Garofalo, Siegel, and Laub (1987) analyzed the National Crime Survey for school-related victimizations among adolescents and found scuffles, threats, and disagreements rather than calculated assaults or violence. Resulting injuries were minor bruises, black eyes, cuts, scratches, and swelling. The picture of school violence was one of teasing, bullying, and horseplay that had gotten out of hand. The researchers determined that the alarm about rampant violence in schools is not justified, but concern about the frequency with which adolescents victimize each other is, even though the victimizations are more bothersome than injurious.

In interpreting the evidence, one can conclude that violence in schools is increasing, but most students are unaffected by it. Those who are tend to overstate its severity. The potential for serious violence is also increasing. Consequently, public concern is justified.

Violence in Society

Violence among young people in society is increasing. Adolescent homicide rates have reached the highest in U.S. history. Gunfire kills 15 individuals under the age of 19 daily. From 1982 to 1992, juvenile arrests for homicides increased 228 percent; the homicide rate among teenage males (15–19 years) more than doubled between 1985 and 1991.

Violence is a growing problem in the workplace. Recent incidences include disgruntled workers killing coworkers at post offices and restaurants. Some estimates place the dollar cost to U.S. businesses for workplace violence at nearly $4.2 billion.

Such an increase in schools and society has led educators to ask, "Why is this violence occurring?" Three influences help answer this question: changing patterns of family and community life; how society has redefined violence as normal and acceptable; and easy access to guns and drugs.

Changing Patterns of Family and Community Life

Today, children are more isolated from parents, extended family members, and other adults than ever before. Workplaces are separated from living places, so children do not see most working adults. Divorce, abuse, poverty, drugs, and other forces that interfere with healthy parenting disrupt many families. With isolation, separation, and abuse comes a lack of socialization. The family, neighborhood, and community dynamics that once socialized young people into the norms of society are often extinct. No one is teaching children how to manage conflicts constructively through example or through indirect methods, such as moral codes and patterns of living.

Some communities directly promote violence as a way to resolve disputes. Inner-city children typically grow up surrounded by teenagers and adults who are themselves deviant, delinquent, or criminal. The result is youth who have been directly and painfully taught to be violent when faced with a conflict.

Redefining Violence as Normal

What is perhaps most alarming is that violence is becoming so commonplace in many communities and schools that it is considered the norm rather than the exception. For example, a 14-year-old girl, responding to her mother's concern about a drive-by shooting near her school, said, "Mom, get used to it—that's the way it is."

Mass media influence how people view violence and deviant behavior. Some television shows obliterate or obscure the boundaries that society has created between good and evil, public and private, shame and pride (Abt and Seesholtz 1994). Politicians and special interest groups may deliberately lie to sell an image or a point of view—actions that have become normal. Killing is sometimes portrayed as understandable and righteous when it advances a certain point of view on a controversial issue.

Easy Access to Guns and Drugs

A combination of guns and drugs results in much of the current violence. Because many young people have easy access to both, conflicts that in the past would have resulted in a bloody lip now result in a deadly shooting. Alcohol and drug use lead to loss of self-control, angry outbursts, and violent acts. A report to Congress tied alcohol to 40 percent of murders and 52 percent of rapes.

What Is the School's Responsibility?

Changes in family, neighborhood, and societal life have resulted in youth who are not socialized into constructive patterns of conflict management and who are taught how to manage conflicts with violence and aggression. Given these circumstances, what is the school's responsibility in teaching students how to be productive and contributing members of our society? How should schools deal with violent and disruptive students? Two views prevail:

• Schools should be places where educators try to salvage lost lives.

• Schools should be places where educators try to maximize the potential of well-behaved students who want an education.

The first view sees the school's mission as saving violent and disruptive students. A report of the National Association of State Boards of Education emphasizes the rights of disruptive students. It also suggests that schools should restructure themselves to provide a curriculum with special programs that teach teachers and students how to cope with violent students. The report proposes that schools bend over backwards *not* to exclude violent or disruptive students or take them out of class. Schools should use alternative programs only when in-class interventions have been exhausted and a plan exists for returning the violent and disruptive students as quickly as possible to their regular classes. The basic position is, *We must not give up on these students, no matter what.*

The second view advocates removing violent and disruptive students from class to increase the quality and quantity of learning for motivated and well-behaved students. Focusing school services and attention on violent students encourages classmates to emulate their behavior. Proponents of this view emphasize requiring students to take responsibility for their behavior by accepting the consequences of their actions. Separating chronically violent and disruptive students from mainstream classes is viewed as the way in which to further the education of all other students.

The argument is over whether schools should teach students how to behave in appropriate and constructive ways or whether schools should teach only students who have already learned how to behave appropriately. The answer is not yet clear. Schools need to be safe havens—concentrating on math is hard if students are apprehensive about their safety.

Making Schools Safe
Learning Environments

Providing students with an orderly environment in which to learn and ensuring student safety are becoming more difficult in many schools. An increasing number of public and private teachers and administrators face situations involving serious conflicts among students and between students and faculty. In response, schools are adopting various violence prevention and conflict resolution programs.

Preventing violence and resolving conflicts are interrelated. Violence prevention programs alone are not enough—students also need to learn how to manage conflicts constructively. Violence and even homicide often result from spontaneous arguments among acquaintances or friends (Prothrow-Stith, Spivak, and Hausman 1987). Students need an alternative to using violence for resolving conflicts.

Training students in conflict resolution not only helps schools become orderly and peaceful places in which high-quality education can take place but also improves instruction. Constructive conflict can gain and hold attention, increase motivation to learn, arouse intellectual curiosity, and improve the quality and creativity of problem solving. The benefits of such training extend beyond schools.

Students are prepared to manage future conflicts constructively in career, family, community, national, and international settings.

To implement violence prevention and conflict resolution programs, schools need to follow a sequential process:

1. Admit that destructive conflicts are out of control.
2. Implement a violence prevention program.
3. Become a conflict positive organization.
4. Implement a conflict resolution program.
   a. Create a cooperative context.
   b. Institute conflict resolution/peer mediation training that teaches students how to negotiate and mediate and teachers how to arbitrate.
   c. Use academic controversy to improve instruction.

2

Violence Prevention

To eliminate violence and resolve destructive conflicts, schools must first admit that such conflicts are out of control. They need to recognize that physical and verbal violence, discipline problems, and incivility are not the work of a few troublemakers or just a passing phase. The next step is to set up a violence prevention program. Most current programs focus on violence prevention only. Schools need a broader context that includes not only measures to prevent violence but also ways to develop and maintain constructive patterns of behavior.

Programs to Prevent Violence

Today's schools are adopting programs to reduce or eliminate violence. Such programs include a variety of components:

• Eliminating weapons brought to schools by installing metal detectors and conducting random searches of lockers.

• Suppressing violent behavior by asking police to patrol schools and arrest students who are violating the law or behaving violently.

• Training faculty and staff on how to recognize and intervene in violent situations.

- Targeting students who commit the most violent acts and using resources to modify their behavior.
- Discrediting violence and increasing status and self-esteem through discussions and role-play.
- Teaching selected students how to recognize and change beliefs that result in violence and how to manage anger.
- Encouraging students to abstain from violence by inviting guest speakers to speak against it.
- Creating a district task force to develop a system for identifying causes of violence.
- Adopting a threat-management policy that assures students they will receive protection if they believe they are in danger.
- Providing debriefing sessions for students traumatized by violent incidences.
- Initiating a weapons hotline that pays students for reporting weapons on the school grounds.

These programs are a good beginning, but they do not go far enough. Their focus is on violence prevention only, and evidence shows that such a limited scope is relatively ineffective. Webster (1993) reviewed evaluations of three current violence prevention curriculums and found no evidence that such programs produce long-term changes in violent behavior or risk of victimization. A survey of 51 violence prevention programs (Wilson-Brewer, Cohen, O'Donnell, and Goodman 1991) shows that less than half claimed to have reduced levels of violence and few had data to support claims of effectiveness. In examining research, Tolan and Guerra (in press) conclude that many schools are engaging in well-intentioned efforts without any evidence that the programs will work. They also found that some programs have negative effects by influencing nonviolent students to be more violence prone.

Studying why this limited focus is ineffective is helping educators develop better programs. Many current programs are poorly targeted. They lump together a broad range of violent behaviors and people, ignoring the fact that people turn to violence for different reasons. Also, few programs concentrate on the small group of students who commit most acts of violence. A study of a peer mediation program in inner-city schools shows that less than five percent of the students accounted for more than one-third of the violent incidents (D.W. Johnson and R. Johnson 1994). Schools should apply resources to helping students who are the most violent.

Some programs are poorly implemented. They assume that a few hours of educational intervention will "cure" violent students, a few hours of training will prepare teachers to conduct the program, and follow-up is not needed. In other words, they are ignoring a valuable source of information—literature on successful innovation within schools.

Programs focusing only on violence prevention sometimes use school settings to try to reduce violence in neighborhood settings. Neighborhoods are often competitive environments where conflicts involve macho posturing, competition for status and power, and access to drugs. Interaction is short term. Schools are cooperative environments where conflicts involve working together, sharing resources, and solving problems. Interaction is long term. Different conflict resolution procedures are required for each setting.

Some programs are unrealistic in assessing the strength of the social forces that result in violence. Schools cannot eliminate the availability of weapons and drugs in society. They cannot change the norms controlling street behavior. Programs need to be realistic in what they can accomplish.

Often, programs are a collection of ideas and procedures that make sense to the authoring practitioner but do not have any grounding in the relevant psychological and sociological theories. Violence prevention should be based on theory and research in violence, aggression, and conflict resolution.

Programs to Prevent Violence and Develop Positive Behavior

Ending school violence is complex. To be successful, programs should have elements that replace violent behavior with nonviolent or positive behavior. The process requires that students change habits, attitudes, values, and perspectives. Comprehensive programs have components that can help effect such change (see Figure 2.1).

Nurturing Needs

Violence prevention begins with good prenatal and postnatal health care for adults and children. Children need good nutrition, adequate housing, and sufficient sleep to help combat the forces that result in violence. Each child also needs to be bonded to a caring adult who is committed to that child's well-being. Strong and healthy relationships help children resist the negative influences of street life. Children must have hope, a reason to believe that they can change the future for themselves and others. They must know that if they work hard and do well in school, they will be able to get a job and have a good life.

Meeting nurturing needs is essential in successful violence prevention programs—but beyond schools' control. Schools can provide the other components.

FIGURE 2.1
Violence Prevention Programs

Violence Prevention Only
Uses One or More Components

Eliminates weapons
Suppresses violent behavior
Trains faculty and staff to intervene
Targets students who commit the most
    violent acts
Discredits violence and increases
    self-esteem
Teaches selected students how to
    manage anger

Encourages students to abstain from
    violence
Creates a district task force to identify
    causes of violence
Adopts a threat-management policy
Provides debriefing sessions for
    students traumatized by violent
    incidents
Initiates a weapons hotline

Comprehensive
Uses All Components

Meets nurturing needs
Creates a cooperative environment
Encourages positive and lasting relationships
Limits out-of-school time
Forms partnerships with parents and community
Provides long-term conflict resolution/peer mediation training
    to all students
Includes components from violence prevention only programs

A Cooperative Environment

Schools can teach children how to cooperate and share. David Hamburg, president of Carnegie Corporation, states that reversing the trend of violence among the young depends on teaching children how to cooperate, share, and help others. He states that the assumption that children are learning these competencies outside school is not sound. Schools should teach children how to work with and be committed to others. One way to create a cooperative school environment is through using cooperative learning for most of the day, organizing teachers into collegial teams committed to improving their instructional expertise, and structuring the school so that the same teachers teach cohorts of students for a number of years (D.W. Johnson and R. Johnson, submitted for publication; D.W. Johnson, Johnson, and Holubec 1993).

Positive and Lasting Relationships

Schools can create positive and lasting bonds among students and between students, faculty, and staff. Children at high risk of violence, academic failure, drug abuse, and dropping out of school often lack a connection to a positive social entity, such as a family, peer group, or church (Posner 1994). By providing dependable and supportive relationships, schools can lessen feelings of estrangement and hopelessness. Positive peer relationships are the keys to psychological health, cognitive and social development, and prosocial attitudes and values (Hartup 1976, Johnson 1981).

Classmates, faculty, and staff are sources of support that students can use to meet personal and academic needs. Structuring relationships that are long term creates a framework for this support. Procedures include forming cooperative learning base groups that last for a number of years (D.W. Johnson, Johnson, and Holubec 1992, 1993) and assigning teams of teachers to follow cohorts of students through several grades (D.W. Johnson and R. Johnson, submitted for publication).

Out-of-School Time

Schools can limit the time children and adolescents have outside school. They can stay open for extracurricular activities on afternoons, evenings, and weekends and during the summer. Keeping students away from the streets, gangs, drugs, and boredom for even a few hours after classes reduces the time that negative influences have to do their work. If schools are to reduce violence, they must provide an alternative place for students to hang out, as well as an alternative set of friends and personal identity.

Partnerships

Schools can form partnerships with parents and the community. Many school officials believe that increases in weapons, fights, gangs, and drug use on school grounds are community problems. Educators cannot hope to solve such problems alone. Increasingly, they are turning to the community for help. Ties are sought with churches, public housing groups, tenant associations, police, businesses, and other community groups.

Educators can conduct classes for parents and students on avoiding threats and family violence, disciplining children, spending more enjoyable time with children, and helping children deal with school problems.

Long-Term Conflict Resolution/Peer Mediation Training

Schools can implement long-term conflict resolution/peer mediation training for all students. It should continue for 12 years and be integrated into the daily patterns of school life.

All students, not a select few, need to learn how to manage conflicts. Everyone—students, faculty, and staff—must use conflict resolution procedures. The school creates its own culture and trains students in how to behave appropriately within that culture. When students and staff enter school grounds, they are expected to use the negotiation and mediation procedures that are central to maintaining the school as a viable learning community.

Habits and attitudes are not changed quickly or easily. Procedures must be taught and retaught, with increasing complexity and sophistication so that students can improve expertise. Competency takes years of practice. It took 30 years to reduce smoking in the United States and 15 years to reduce drunk driving—reducing violence may take even longer.

3

Schools as Conflict Positive Organizations

If civilization is to survive, we must cultivate the science of human relationships—the ability of all peoples, of all kinds, to live together, in the same world at peace.

—Franklin Delano Roosevelt

Conflicts occur all the time. They are a normal and inevitable part of school life. Students disagree over who to sit by at lunch, which game to play during recess, when to work and when to play, when to talk and when to listen, and who is going to pick the paper up off the floor. How conflicts are managed, not their presence, determines if they are destructive or constructive. Conflict negative schools manage conflicts destructively; conflict positive schools manage conflicts constructively. Unfortunately, most schools today are conflict negative; they should aspire to be conflict positive.

Conflict Negative Schools

Conflict negative schools assume that all conflicts are destructive and have no value. Management goals, therefore, are to try to eliminate them by suppressing, avoiding, and denying their existence. The effects of unavoidable conflicts are minimized. When cornered into a conflict, participants try to win. Conflicts are a source of problems, producing fear, anxiety, insecurity, and defensiveness. Avoidance procedures include isolating or separating potentially disruptive people. Conflict negative schools do not teach students, faculty, and staff how to manage conflicts because such training might encourage conflicts.

Conflict Positive Schools

Conflict positive schools manage conflicts constructively to enhance the quality of teaching, learning, and school life. They recognize that conflicts are inevitable, healthy, and valuable. Conflicts are not problems—they are part of solutions. Faculty and administration create and encourage the possibility of conflict, which produces feelings of excitement, interest, and a sense of promise. They organize students and faculty into teams: Students work in cooperative learning groups, and faculty work in collegial teaching teams. The teams are trained in how to use specific procedures, so that everyone is operating from the same knowledge base.

To create conflict positive schools, educators first need a general understanding of conflict. Then they need to apply that understanding within the context of a school environment (see Figure 3.1).

FIGURE 3.1
Creating Conflict Positive Schools: What Educators Should Know

What conflict is
Destructive and constructive conflicts
Value of conflict
Need for coorientation and a conflict resolution program

What Is a Conflict?

A conflict can be as small as a disagreement or as large as a war. Deutsch (1973) probably defines it best: A conflict exists when incompatible activities occur. One incompatible activity prevents or interferes with the occurrence or effectiveness of a second activity. These activities may originate in one person, between two or more people, or between two or more groups.

The interests of students, teachers, and administrators are sometimes congruent and sometimes in conflict. A conflict of interests occurs when the actions of one person attempting to reach his or her goals prevent or interfere with the actions of another person attempting to reach his or her goals (Deutsch 1973). Conflicts of interests are common—they occur naturally and are deliberately created. In many classrooms, teachers set up a conflict of interests among students by having them compete for grades. To learn how to resolve conflicts of interests, educators need to understand the meaning of wants, needs, goals, and interests (D.W. Johnson and R. Johnson 1991). Figure 3.2 provides definitions of these terms.

FIGURE 3.2
Definitions of Conflict Resolution Terms

Term	Definition
Want	A desire for something.
Need	A necessity for survival.
Goal	An ideal state that we value and work to achieve.
Interest	A potential benefit to be gained by achieving goals.
Conflict of interests	A situation in which the actions of one person interfere with or block those of another person attempting to reach his goals.

Destructive and Constructive Conflicts

Conflicts can become destructive when they are denied, suppressed, or avoided. If students do not have conflict management training, they will use their own techniques, which are often inadequate. They may get angry, fight, and harass or abuse each other verbally. Such actions do not usually resolve problems and often result in alienating students from their peers and faculty. Destructive conflicts can destroy effectiveness, rip apart relationships, sabotage work, delay and decrease teaching and learning efforts, and devastate individual commitment to an organization's goals (Janz and Tjosvold 1985).

History is filled with exciting examples of constructive conflicts. One example is the conflict between the Federalists and anti-Federalists, which resulted in the Bill of Rights in the U.S. Constitution. Well-managed conflicts offer an opportunity to see a problem more clearly, acquire new ideas, and motivate change for the better. Figure 3.3 summarizes the differences between the two types of conflict.

FIGURE 3.3
Types of Conflict

Destructive	Constructive
One participant wins at the other's expense.	All participants achieve their goals.
Participants are angry, resentful, hurt, and distrustful.	Participants like, respect, and trust each other more.
Possibility of constructively resolving future conflicts with each other decreases.	Potential to resolve constructively future conflicts with each other increases.

Value of Conflict

Constructively managed conflicts have many positive outcomes (Deutsch 1973; Johnson 1970; D.W. Johnson and F. Johnson 1994; D.W. Johnson and R. Johnson 1979, 1991). Conflicts can improve achievement, reasoning, and problem solving. They help young people mature. Taking another person's perspective helps adolescents become less egocentric. They also learn about themselves— what makes them angry, what frightens them, what is important to them.

Confidence in their skills encourages students to become more cooperative and involved. The more students learn about how to take a cooperative approach to managing conflicts, the healthier they tend to be psychologically. They are better able to deal with stress and adversity.

Conflicts are energizing. They can trigger physical energy and an intense psychological focus. This energy motivates individuals to resolve the conflict and put their plans into action. People sometimes seek out conflicts through such activities as competitive sports and games, because the interactions are stimulating and fun.

Learning conflict management skills and understanding the importance of being part of a cooperative team make students more employable. They can maintain higher quality relationships with superiors, peers, and subordinates in the workplace.

Conflict can deepen a relationship, strengthening each person's conviction that the relationship can hold up under stress. Resolving a conflict creates a sense of joint identity and cohesiveness. Nothing divides humans more than poorly managed conflicts. Nothing brings humans together more than constructively managed conflicts.

Conflicts make us aware of problems that need to be solved. Recognizing that a problem exists, who is involved, and how we can solve it helps reduce the irritations of relating to others.

Coorientation

> If we are to reach real peace in the world we shall have to begin with children; and if they will grow up in their natural innocence, we won't have to struggle; we won't have to pass fruitless ideal resolutions, but we shall go from love to love and peace to peace, until at last all the corners of the world are covered with the peace and love for which consciously or unconsciously the whole world is hungering.
>
> —Mohandas Gandhi

Students have different ideas about how to resolve conflicts. Some rely on physical dominance through threats and violence. Others use verbal attack, the cold shoulder, giving in, or getting back at the other person. Multiple procedures can create chaos within a classroom. This chaos can be reduced if students and staff are cooriented so that they operate under the same norms and follow the same conflict resolution procedures.

Norms are shared expectations about what behavior is appropriate within a situation. Conflict resolution begins with a common set of norms, which must be clearly and publicly established. For example, physical violence against oneself or another person, public humiliation and shaming, and lying and deceit should be outlawed.

Ensuring that all students use the same procedures is especially important when students are from different cultures, ethnic groups, and linguistic backgrounds. While this diversity represents a source of creativity and energy, it also may provide problems in managing classroom conflicts. Suspicions and fears may need to be eliminated. Differences may need to be recognized and accommodated.

Students and staff become cooriented through a conflict resolution program that sets up a cooperative environment, institutes resolution and mediation training, and uses academic controversies to improve instruction. Such a program is primarily established and maintained day-to-day by classroom teachers.

4

Conflict Resolution

P eople have been resolving conflicts constructively for a long time. Ancient civilizations used a variety of methods, and today we continue to draw upon diverse resources to develop school programs with different emphases and approaches. Exploring the history of conflict resolution helps us understand the makeup of a comprehensive conflict resolution program. Such a program has three parts:

• Creating a cooperative context (see Chapter 5).
• Instituting conflict resolution/peer mediation training (see Chapters 7–10).
• Using academic controversy to improve instruction (see Chapter 11).

History

Modern conflict resolution programs stress peer mediation, a technique found in many cultures. In ancient China, people practiced the Confucian way of resolving disputes by using moral persuasion and agreement. In Japan, the village leader was expected to use mediation and conciliation to help community members settle their disputes. In parts of Africa, a neighborhood meeting, or "moot," assembled, and a respected member helped disputants resolve their conflict without involving a judge or arbitrator and without using sanctions. In some cultures, members of extended families served as mediators. For centuries, local religious leaders, such as priests, ministers, and rabbis, were community mediators.

Even though community mediation has been a part of societal living for thousands of years, school-based programs are relatively young, spanning three decades. They have evolved from four general sources: researchers in the field of conflict resolution; groups committed to nonviolence, such as the Quaker Church; opponents of nuclear war; and lawyers. Recently, groups concerned about the rising frequency of violence among children and teenagers have also developed programs.

Teaching Students to Be Peacemakers Program

One of the first conflict resolution and peer mediation programs was Teaching Students to Be Peacemakers, developed in the mid-1960s at the University of Minnesota (Johnson 1970, 1972/1993, 1978/1991; D.W. Johnson and F. Johnson 1975/1994; D.W. Johnson, Johnson, and Johnson 1976). David Johnson and other researchers translated conflict resolution theory and the results of ongoing research into a set of practical procedures. Building positive relationships among disputants is a major focus.

The peacemaker program is part of a larger approach that uses a cooperative context and academic controversies to train all students to negotiate their conflicts and mediate peer conflicts. An assumption is that all students are empowered to regulate their own behavior and resolve their interpersonal conflicts constructively. Chapter 10 discusses how to implement the peacemaker program.

Children's Creative Response to Conflict Program

In the early 1970s, Quaker teachers in New York City became interested in providing nonviolence training to children. Their efforts resulted in the founding of the Children's Creative Response to Conflict (CCRC). Priscilla Prutzman was the program's first director. Public school workshops show teachers how to help children learn the skills of creative conflict resolution.

CCRC's roots originate in the teachings of Gandhi and Martin Luther King Jr. Advocates believe that the power of nonviolence lies in the force of justice, the power of love and caring, and the desire for personal integrity. Such programs are based on the assumption that if peace is what every government seeks, and peace is the yearning of every heart, then we should study and teach it in our schools.

Resolving Conflict Creatively Program

Preventing nuclear war and advocating peace and global education were the guiding principles for Educators for Social Responsibility (ESR), a national organization founded in the early 1980s. ESR's interests led them to address violence in classrooms. In partnership with the New York City public schools, ESR began the Resolving Conflict Creatively Program. Schools implement a curriculum with lessons on intergroup relations, cooperative learning, and dispute resolution procedures; provide peer mediation training; and conduct workshops for parents.

Community Boards of San Francisco Conflict Managers Program

In 1977, trial lawyer Ray Shonholtz responded to President Carter's call for Neighborhood Justice Centers by establishing the Community Boards of San Francisco Conflict Managers Program. Initially, mediators taught conflict resolution skills to adults in neighborhoods. Then they approached local schools about beginning a peer mediation program. Conflict management curriculums were subsequently developed and implemented in elementary, middle, and high schools.

Two Approaches

School conflict resolution programs can generally be described as using either a cadre or a total student body approach. The cadre approach emphasizes training a small number of students to serve as peer mediators. The Community Boards of San Francisco Conflict Managers Program is an example. Proponents believe that a few specially trained students can defuse and constructively resolve interpersonal conflicts that occur among members of the student body. Training usually consists of a one- to two-day workshop or a semester-long class. The cadre approach is relatively easy and inexpensive for a school to adopt. Its effectiveness, however, has not been clearly demonstrated.

The total student body approach emphasizes training every student to manage conflicts constructively (D.W. Johnson and R. Johnson 1991). The Teaching Students to Be Peacemakers Program is an example. Because training all students and staff in the same negotiation and mediation procedures requires considerable time and commitment, the program is relatively costly.

Conflict Resolution as a Discipline Program

Discipline problems disrupt the cooperative nature of schools. To deal with these problems, schools institute discipline programs, which can be placed on a continuum. At one end are programs based on adult-administered external rewards and punishments. Faculty control and manage student behavior. At the other end are programs based on teaching students the competencies and skills required for them to manage their own and their schoolmates' behavior. Peer mediation programs anchor the self-regulation end of the continuum (see Figure 4.1).

FIGURE 4.1

Continuum for Discipline Programs

External Rewards/Punishments ----------------------------------▶ Self-Regulation

Most discipline programs are clustered at the external rewards/punishments end. Staff monitor student behavior, determine whether it is within the bounds of acceptability, and force students to terminate inappropriate actions. When infractions are minor, staff often arbitrate: "The pencil belongs to Mary. Robert, be quiet and sit down." They may also cajole students to end hostilities: "Let's forgive and forget. Shake hands and be friends." If these methods do not work, students may be sent to the principal's office for a stern but cursory lecture about the value of getting along, a threat that if the conflict continues more drastic action will ensue, and a final admonition to "Go and fight no more." If visiting the principal does not work, time-out rooms may be used. Eventually, some students are expelled.

Programs that use external rewards and punishments teach students that adults or authority figures are needed to resolve conflicts. Such programs work only as long as students are under surveillance. Instructional and administrative time is costly. This approach does not empower students. Adults may become more skillful in how to control students, but students do not learn the procedures, skills, and attitudes required to resolve conflicts constructively in their personal lives at home, in school, at work, and in the community.

Programs at the other end of the continuum teach students self-regulation, the ability to act in socially approved ways in the absence of external monitors. Students learn to initiate and cease activities according to situational demands. Self-regulation is a hallmark of cognitive and social development. To regulate their behavior, students first must monitor it, assess situations, and take other people's perspectives so that they can judge which behaviors are appropriate. They then must master the procedures and skills required to engage in the desired behaviors.

If students are to learn how to regulate their behavior, they must have opportunities to make decisions on how to behave and follow through on the decisions. Allowing students to be joint architects in issues affecting them promotes feelings of control and autonomy. Ideally, students should be given the responsibility of regulating their own and their classmates' behavior so that teachers can concentrate on instruction rather than on control.

The types of discipline problems occurring in a school help determine what type of discipline program to implement. Typically, most problems involve conflicts among people or conflicts about standards of appropriate conduct. Students can be trained to manage these types of conflicts.

5

Creating a Cooperative Context

The best way I know how to defeat an enemy is to make him a friend.

—Abraham Lincoln

Two possible contexts for conflict exist: cooperative and competitive. Teaching students to manage conflicts constructively makes little sense if a school is structured competitively. Students are working in a competitive environment when they compete for scarce rewards (e.g., teacher attention and high grades) and have to defeat each other to get what they want. Rewards are restricted to the few who perform the best (D.W. Johnson and R. Johnson 1989). Competitors typically have a short-term time orientation and focus their energies on winning. They are not interested in maintaining good, long-term relationships. Competitors tend to avoid communicating with each other, misperceive each other's position and motivations, view each other with suspicion, deny the legitimacy of others' needs and feelings, and see the situation only from their perspective.

The seminal work of Morton Deutsch (1973) demonstrates that to resolve conflicts constructively, a cooperative context must be established. All participants are committed to achieving mutual goals

(Deutsch 1973, D.W. Johnson and R. Johnson 1989). Cooperators tend to seek outcomes that are beneficial to everyone involved. They typically have a long-term time orientation and focus their energies both on achieving goals and maintaining good working relationships. Communication is frequent, complete, and truthful, with each person interested in informing and being informed. Cooperative people usually perceive accurately other participants' positions and motivations. Since cooperators trust and like one another, they are usually willing to respond to each other's wants, needs, and requests. Cooperators recognize the legitimacy of the other's interests and search for a solution that can accommodate all sides.

Cooperative Learning

Educators create a cooperative context by structuring a majority of learning situations cooperatively (D.W. Johnson and R. Johnson 1989; D.W. Johnson, Johnson, and Holubec 1993). Students work in small groups to accomplish shared learning goals. They have two responsibilities: to learn the assigned material and ensure that all other group members also learn it. Cooperative learning uses a criteria-based evaluation system in which student achievement is judged against a fixed set of standards. Students who achieve the standards pass; those who do not, fail. Three types of cooperative learning help students achieve shared goals: formal cooperative learning, informal cooperative learning, and cooperative base groups.

Formal Cooperative Learning

In formal cooperative learning, students work together for one class period to several weeks to reach their goals and complete specific tasks, such as making decisions, solving problems, completing a curriculum unit, writing a report, conducting a survey or experiment, reading a chapter or reference book, learning vocabulary, or answering questions at the end of a chapter. Any course requirement or assignment can be reformulated to be cooperative. Teachers have five responsibilities (D.W. Johnson, Johnson, and Holubec 1993):

1. Specify the lesson objectives. Every lesson has two objectives: The academic objective states the concepts and strategies to be

learned; the social skills objective states the interpersonal or small-group skill to be mastered.

2. Make preinstructional decisions. Teachers decide the group sizes, method of assigning students to groups, student roles, materials needed, and room arrangement.

3. Explain the task and the positive interdependence for that task. Teachers define an assignment, teach the required concepts and strategies, specify the positive interdependence (discussed in this chapter in "What Makes Cooperative Learning Work?") and individual accountability, give the criteria for success, and explain the expected social skills.

4. Monitor student learning and intervene if necessary. Teachers systematically observe and collect data on each group. When needed, they intervene to help students complete the task accurately and work together effectively.

5. Evaluate student learning and help students evaluate their groups. Teachers first assess learning and performance, then help group members process how effectively they have been working together.

Informal Cooperative Learning

Informal cooperative learning uses temporary, ad hoc groups that last from a few minutes to one class period to achieve a shared goal (D.W. Johnson, Johnson, and Holubec 1992; D.W. Johnson, Johnson, and Smith 1991). During a lecture, demonstration, or film, this type of group can focus student attention on the material to be learned, set a mood conducive to learning, help develop expectations about what will be covered in a class session, ensure that students cognitively process the material, and provide closure. Teachers may organize groups so that students engage in focused discussions (three to five minutes) before and after a lecture and turn-to-your-partner discussions (one to two minutes) interspersed throughout a lecture.

Cooperative Base Groups

Cooperative base groups are long-term (one to several years), heterogeneous learning groups with a stable membership (D.W. Johnson, Johnson, and Holubec 1992; D.W. Johnson, Johnson, and Smith 1991). The purpose is to provide the support needed for each member to progress academically and develop cognitively and socially. Base groups meet daily in elementary school and usually twice a week in secondary school (whenever the class meets). Members discuss each person's academic progress, assist one another, and verify that each is completing assignments and progressing satisfactorily. They may also inform absent group members about work that was missed. Such an environment provides opportunities for caring peer relationships that influence individuals to work hard. Base groups improve attendance, personalize work and the school experience, and improve the quality and quantity of learning.

What Makes Cooperative Learning Work?

Simply placing students in groups and telling them to work together does not always result in cooperative outcomes. Group efforts can go wrong, such as competition at close quarters or unnecessary talking. To implement cooperative learning successfully, educators need to understand the essential elements of cooperation (D.W. Johnson and R. Johnson 1989):

• Positive Interdependence. Positive interdependence is students' perception that they are linked together so that one cannot succeed unless everyone succeeds. It promotes a situation in which students maximize the learning of all group members, sharing resources, providing mutual support, and celebrating joint successes. Positive interdependence is the heart of cooperative learning. Students must believe that they sink or swim together. Teachers can use several methods to structure positive interdependence in a learning group:

◊ Group Goal. Specifying a group goal that requires all members work together to achieve it. An example is setting the goal for all group members to write a composition that meets the criteria the teacher has specified.

◊ Joint Rewards. For example, awarding five bonus points to each group member if all members score 90 percent or higher correctly on a test.

◊ Divided Resources. For example, giving each group member a part of the total information required to complete an assignment.

◊ Complementary Roles. Assigning roles whose actions help the group complete the joint task. For example, an "encourager" ensures that all members participate; a "checker" ensures that all members can explain how to reach a conclusion (D.W. Johnson, Johnson, and Holubec 1994).

• Individual Accountability. Individual accountability exists when teachers assess each student's performance and give the results to the group and the individual. Groups should be informed about who needs more help and encouragement and also understand that they cannot "hitchhike" on the work of others.

The purpose of cooperative learning groups is to make each member a stronger individual. Students learn together so that they can subsequently perform better separately. To ensure that each member is strengthened, students are accountable to do their share of the work. Common ways to structure individual accountability include the following:

◊ Testing each student individually.

◊ Randomly selecting one student's product to represent the entire group.

◊ Asking students to explain what they have learned to classmates.

• Face-to-Face Promotive Interaction. Once teachers have established positive interdependence, they need to maximize the opportunity for students to promote each other's efforts to learn. Some cognitive activities and interpersonal dynamics occur only when students are involved in this type of activity. Students can help group members by explaining how to solve problems, discussing the concepts they are learning, and sharing knowledge. Accountability to peers, ability to influence each other's reasoning and conclusions, social modeling, social support, and interpersonal rewards increase as face-to-face interaction among group members increases. Promoting each other's success results in higher achievement and better relationships. Meaningful face-to-face interaction is most successful in small groups of two to four students.

• Social Skills. Contributing to the success of a cooperative effort requires interpersonal and small-group skills. Skills in leadership, decision making, trust building, communication, and conflict management have to be taught just as purposefully and precisely as academic skills. Procedures and strategies for teaching social skills are found in work by D.W. Johnson (1972/1993, 1978/1991) and D.W. Johnson and F. Johnson (1994).

• Group Processing. Group processing occurs when members discuss how well they are achieving their goals and maintaining effective working relationships. Groups describe what actions are helpful and unhelpful and decide what behaviors to continue or change. Such processing enables students to focus on group maintenance; aids the learning of social skills; and ensures that members receive feedback on their participation. Keys to successful processing are allowing sufficient time for it to take place, making it specific rather than vague, maintaining student involvement, reminding students to use social skills during processing, and ensuring that the purpose of processing has been clearly communicated.

The Cooperative School

Willi Unsoeld, a renowned mountain climber and philosopher, once stated, "Take care of each other. Share your energies with the group. No one must feel alone, cut off, for that is when you do not make it." The same may be said of everyone in schools. The issue of cooperation among students is part of a larger issue of schools' organizational structure. This structure uses a mass-production model that business and industry have followed for decades. Such a model divides work into small component parts. Individuals work separately from and sometimes in competition with peers. Personnel are considered interchangeable parts. In schools, the component parts are grades (e.g., 1st, 2nd, and 3rd) and subjects (e.g., English, math, and science). Teachers work alone, in their own room, with their own set of students, and with their own set of curriculum materials. Students can be assigned to any teacher, because teachers are considered interchangeable parts; conversely, teachers can be given any student to teach. Schools need to change from a mass-production, competitive, individualistic structure to a high-performance, cooperative, team-based one (D.W. Johnson and F. Johnson 1994). The new structure is known as the cooperative school.

Cooperative schools need implementation at three levels: classroom, school, and district. The organizational structure at these levels is then congruent, each supporting and enhancing the others.

Using cooperative learning a majority of the time in the classroom creates positive relationships among students and improves their level of achievement and psychological well-being. Such an environment also affects teachers' attitudes and competencies. Teachers usually cannot promote isolation and competition among students all day and be collaborative with colleagues. What is promoted in instructional situations tends to dominate relationships among staff members.

Cooperative teams for school staff can be collegial support groups, task forces, and ad hoc decision-making teams (D.W. Johnson and F. Johnson 1994). Support groups consist of two to five teachers whose purpose is to increase members' instructional expertise and success. Faculty meetings use task forces and ad hoc decision-making teams to involve everyone in important decisions. Task forces consider issues ranging from curriculum adoptions to lunchroom behavior. They gather data and present recommendations at faculty meetings. Staff then divide into small decision-making teams to discuss the recommendations; the teams report their decisions to the entire faculty who decides what actions to take.

District-level administrators can use collegial support groups to increase their administrative expertise and success. Implementing task forces, shared decision making, and cooperative procedures also help promote a cooperative environment.

Decreasing Inschool Risk Factors

Cooperative learning decreases risk factors that influence children and adolescents to use violence and other destructive strategies in managing conflicts. Poor academic performance, alienation from schoolmates, and psychological pathology are three risk factors. The more schools do to reduce them, the less violence and destructively managed conflicts schools should experience.

Students who fail academically are more at risk than students who achieve. Sociologists have identified patterns of school-induced delinquency caused by school failure. Unable to secure self-esteem in positive ways, some students seek status through antisocial behavior. A cooperative context helps increase self-esteem by ensuring that every student achieves up to his or her ability. The more students know and the better they can analyze situations, the more able they will be to envision the consequences of their actions, understand and respect differing viewpoints, conceive strategies for dealing with conflict, and engage in creative problem solving.

Students who are alienated from their schoolmates are more at risk than students who are integrated into caring and supportive relationships in schools. Healthy human attachments usually originate from parents who teach trust, competence, and prosocial behavior. Peer relationships are also a powerful influence. Schools promote long-term, caring relationships through cooperative learning and assigning teams of teachers to follow cohorts of students through several grades.

Children and adolescents who have high levels of psychological pathology are more at risk than students who are psychologically well adjusted. Because cooperative learning promotes psychological health, self-esteem, social competencies, and resilience in the face of adversity and stress, students will be less likely to use violence and other destructive strategies in managing their conflicts.

Outcomes of Cooperation

Experimental and correlational studies conducted during the past 90 years show that learning together can profoundly affect students. Researchers compared the relative effects of cooperative, competitive, and individualistic efforts on instructional outcomes (see D.W. Johnson and R. Johnson [1989] for a complete listing and review of these studies). Their findings identified numerous outcomes, which they classified into three general categories:

• Cooperative learning promotes greater effort to achieve.

• Cooperative learning experiences promote more positive relationships among students.

• Cooperative learning experiences result in greater psychological adjustment, self-esteem, and social competence.

If future generations are to manage conflicts constructively, they must be taught the necessary procedures and skills. Experts on organizations constantly remind us that behavior is 85 percent determined by organizational structure and 15 percent determined by the individual (D.W. Johnson and F. Johnson 1994). The first step in teaching students how to manage conflicts is to create a cooperative context (see Figure 5.1) where they learn how to define conflicts as mutual problems to be resolved in ways that benefit everyone involved. Once this context is established, students can be taught negotiation, mediation, and academic controversy procedures.

FIGURE 5.1
Creating a Cooperative School Environment to Resolve Conflicts

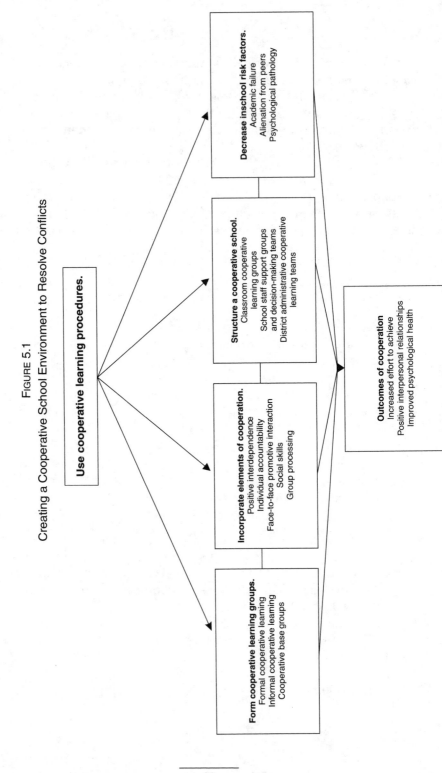

Use cooperative learning procedures.

Form cooperative learning groups.
Formal cooperative learning
Informal cooperative learning
Cooperative base groups

Incorporate elements of cooperation.
Positive interdependence
Individual accountability
Face-to-face promotive interaction
Social skills
Group processing

Structure a cooperative school.
Classroom cooperative learning groups
School staff support groups and decision-making teams
District administrative cooperative learning teams

Decrease inschool risk factors.
Academic failure
Alienation from peers
Psychological pathology

Outcomes of cooperation
Increased effort to achieve
Positive interpersonal relationships
Improved psychological health

6

Two Basic Concerns in a Conflict

I hold it to be a proof of great prudence for men to abstain from threats and insulting words toward anyone, for neither . . . diminishes the strength of the enemy; but the one makes him more cautious, and the other increases his hatred of you and makes him more persevering in his efforts to injure you.

—Niccolo Machiavelli

Dealing with a conflict is like going swimming in a cold lake. Some people like to test the water, sticking their foot in and entering slowly. They want to get used to the cold gradually. Others like to take a running start and leap in. They want to get the cold shock over with quickly. Similarly, different people use different strategies for managing conflicts. Usually, we learn these strategies in childhood, so that later they seem to function automatically on a "preconscious" level. We do whatever seems to come naturally. But we do have a personal strategy and because we learned it, we can always change it by learning new and more effective ways of managing conflicts.

Within any conflict, we need to consider two concerns (D.W. Johnson and R. Johnson 1991):

- Achieving a goal (also called concern for self).
- Maintaining an appropriate relationship with the other person (also called concern for others).

Understanding the relative importance of these concerns helps in choosing the most effective conflict strategy and applying basic rules for resolving conflicts.

Strategies for Managing Conflicts

How important your goal is to you and how important the relationship is affect how you manage a conflict. Placing them on a continuum ranging from not important to highly important may help in determining their relative importance. Where you put them can help you decide which conflict strategy best suits your situation. Five possible strategies can be used.

Problem-Solving Negotiations

When both the goal and the relationship are highly important, you initiate problem-solving negotiations. You seek solutions that ensure that you and the other person fully achieve both goals and resolve any tensions and negative feelings. You maintain your interests and try to find a way of reconciling them with the other's interests. This strategy requires risky moves, such as revealing your underlying interests and expecting the other to do the same. Problem-solving negotiations are discussed in Chapter 7.

Smoothing

When the goal is not important but the relationship is highly important, you give up your goal to maintain the relationship at the highest quality possible. Smoothing is a good idea when a colleague feels strongly about something and you do not. Smooth with good humor. At times, you may need to apologize. Saying "I'm sorry" does not mean "I'm wrong." It lets the other person know that you are sorry about the situation.

Forcing or Win-Lose Negotiations

When the goal is highly important but the relationship is not, you seek to achieve your goal by forcing or persuading the other to yield. You compete for a win by engaging in win-lose negotiations. For example, when buying a used car, you concentrate on spending as little money as possible, regardless of how the salesperson feels. In a tennis match, you may try to win without regard for how the other person feels about being defeated. Tactics to force the other to yield include making threats, imposing penalties that will be withdrawn if the other concedes, and taking preemptive actions designed to resolve the conflict without the other's consent (e.g., taking a book home that the other insists is his). Tactics to persuade the other to yield include presenting persuasive arguments, imposing a deadline, committing oneself to an unalterable position, or making demands that far exceed what is actually acceptable.

Compromising

When both the goal and the relationship are moderately important and you and the other person cannot seem to get what both want, you may need to give up part of your goal and sacrifice part of the relationship to reach an agreement. Compromising may involve meeting in the middle so each gets half or flipping a coin to let chance decide who will get his or her way. Disputants often compromise when they wish to engage in problem-solving negotiations but do not have the time to do so.

Withdrawing

When the goal is not important and you do not need to keep a relationship with the other person, you may wish to give up both and avoid the issue and the person. For example, avoiding a hostile stranger may be the best action to take. Sometimes you may wish to withdraw from a conflict until you and the other person have calmed down and can control your feelings.

Feasibility

For you to choose a strategy, you must believe that it will work. You are more likely to use one when certain conditions exist:

• Problem-Solving Negotiations. You recognize that the positive interdependence between you and the other person is increasing; the potential for finding alternatives that will allow both of you to achieve your goals is increasing; and you and the other person trust each other and are confident that you each have the required skills.

• Smoothing. The other person's interests seem more important than yours, the other person has recently engaged in smoothing in your relationship, and time is very short.

• Forcing or Win-Lose Negotiations. You see the relationship as temporary and the other person's willingness to smooth or yield is increasing.

• Compromising. You and the other person's commitment to each's own interests is decreasing and time pressures are increasing.

• Withdrawing. You think the relationship is ending and the other person seems irrational and unable to solve the problem.

Points to Consider

• You must be competent in each strategy, practicing all of them until they are mastered. You do not want to be an overspecialized dinosaur who can deal with conflict in only one way. Each strategy is appropriate under a certain set of conditions, and based on your goal and the relationship with the other person, you choose the conflict strategy appropriate to the situation.

• Some strategies require the participation of the other disputant, and some may be enacted alone. You can give up your goals by withdrawing and smoothing, no matter what the other disputant does. When you try to achieve your goals by forcing, compromising, and problem solving, the other disputant has to participate in the process.

• The strategies tend to be incompatible—choosing one makes choosing the others less likely. Withdrawing implies lack of commitment to one's goals, and negotiating implies high commitment. Sometimes, however, these two strategies can be combined, such as temporarily withdrawing before initiating negotiations. Forcing implies low commitment to the relationship, and smoothing implies high commitment.

• Certain strategies may deteriorate into other strategies. When you try to withdraw and the other disputant pursues you and will not allow you to withdraw, you may respond with forcing. When you initiate problem-solving negotiations and the other disputant responds with forcing, you may reciprocate by engaging in win-lose tactics. When time is short, problem-solving negotiations may deteriorate into compromising.

• Your perception of the relationship's future determines whether you initiate problem-solving or win-lose negotiations. Potential short-term gains must be weighed against potential long-term losses. When you believe the relationship is unimportant, you may go for a win by trying to force the other person to capitulate. Limited interactions with the other person or anger may make the relationship seem unimportant. When you believe the relationship is important, you try to solve the problem in a way that achieves the other person's goals as well as your own. Strong positive emotions (such as liking and respect) or a relationship that is ongoing and long term bonds you to the other person, making the relationship important.

When individuals realize they will work with each other frequently and for a long time (such as a year or more), they see that the long-term benefits of cooperation outweigh the short-term benefits of taking advantage of the other person. In other words, the future outweighs the present. The quality of the relationship is more important than the outcome of the negotiation. Most school relationships are ongoing and long term; therefore, the shadow of the future is ever present.

Rules to Resolve Conflicts

Because long-term relationships are highly important in schools, knowing how to manage conflicts to maintain those relationships is essential. The following rules can be used as guidelines.

Do Not Withdraw from or Ignore a Conflict

In headaches and in worry
Vaguely life leaks away.

—W.H. Auden

When a long-term relationship is involved, face a conflict and openly negotiate constructive resolutions. In addition to possibly damaging the relationship, ignoring a conflict has personal costs:

• Keeps emotional energy tied up in fear, resentment, and hostility. For example, repressing anger may lead to emotional explosions that create new conflicts and revive old ones in destructive ways.

• Causes emotions such as anger, resentment, fear, and dislike to be expressed indirectly. For example, anger can become sulkiness, uncooperativeness, sarcasm, or talking behind the other person's back. New conflicts are created, incurring further costs.

• Results in the conflict being dealt with indirectly. Conflicts handled indirectly have the longest life expectancy and the most costs (often seemingly unrelated to the original conflict).

Withdrawing is appropriate only when your goal is not important and you do not need to keep a relationship with the other person. You give up your goal and the relationship. The procedure for withdrawing is to avoid the other person or refuse to talk about the issue.

You may wish to withdraw for various reasons (Johnson 1978/ 1991), D.W. Johnson and R. Johnson 1991). You may not know the other person or care about the issue. You may be afraid of potential social isolation, humiliation, and loss of status as friends and school-mates become involved and choose sides. You may fear that if you express your anger or resentment you will be disliked, rejected, attacked, or seen as a complainer. Facing a conflict and attempting to resolve it carries the risk of creating a residue of interpersonal antagonisms that may hurt your social status in the school. Based on experience, you may believe trying to resolve the conflict is hopeless. When a person has continually experienced negative outcomes in conflict situations, a state of learned helplessness results in which the person believes that nothing he or she can do will create a positive resolution of a conflict (Seligman 1975). Consequently, withdrawing physically and psychologically seems easier. You may be inhibited from expressing anger, resentment, or envy because you consider such actions bad manners or immature. Temporarily withdrawing from and ignoring a conflict may be constructive so that you can confront the other person at a more advantageous time or deal with the conflict when more information is available.

Do Not Engage in Win-Lose Negotiations

I know I am among civilized men because they are fighting so savagely.

—Voltaire

Engaging in win-lose negotiations is inappropriate in a school environment. Remember the adage, "Never walk away with a win;

keep negotiating until the other person and you both have what you want. If you walk away with a win, you will have to watch your back every time you pass a dark doorway, and life is too short to be constantly watching your back!"

Forcing assumes that conflicts are settled when one person wins and the other person loses. The strategy is to take an extreme opening position and adopt a slow rate of compromise in an attempt to force the other person to concede. You may supplement this strategy with persuasive arguments, threats, and attacks aimed at overpowering, overwhelming, or intimidating others. When you force, you seek to achieve your goals, without concern for the goals of others or their feelings toward you.

If you win, you may damage the relationship. Forcing usually creates resistance and resentment and reduces the likelihood of working together effectively in the future. Reactance theory (Brehm 1966) predicts that any attempt to reduce someone's perceived freedom or control will motivate that person to reassert freedom or control. In other words, the harder you push the other person to give in, the harder the other person will push back. The more you force, the more the other person resists and the angrier the other person becomes. When forcing is successful, winning may result in a sense of pride and achievement. When it is unsuccessful, it may result in depression, guilt, shame, and failure. Forcing always carries a high risk of alienating the other person and starting a spiral of win-lose tactics. Others may censure you.

Forcing can develop inadvertently. In negotiations, you and the other person each take a position, argue for it, and make concessions to reach a compromise or search for a mutually beneficial solution. The process involves successively taking then giving up a sequence of positions. The danger is that individuals may lock themselves into the positions they are taking. The more you clarify your position and defend it against attack, the more committed you become to it. The more you try to convince the other person of the impossibility of changing your position, the more difficult it becomes for you to do so. Your ego becomes identified with your position. You may become more interested in saving face than in seeking a wise agreement. In defending your position and trying to win, you may pay less attention to meeting the underlying concerns of the other person. Agreement becomes less likely. Avoid the temptation to attempt to force the other person to adopt a position that lets you win.

Assess for Smoothing

A soft answer turneth away wrath.

—Bible

Smoothing involves letting the other person have his or her way. You may wish to smooth when you care more about the relationship than the goal. When relationships are long term, each person is concerned about the other's interests. The quality of one life depends at least partially on the quality of the relationship maintained with the other person. Appropriate smoothing occurs when two people share mutual long-term goals. They accurately and clearly present their wants and interests and weigh those interests to determine whose are stronger or more important. One person then gives up his or her interests to help the other.

Smoothing only works if it is reciprocal. Over time, the wants and interests of each person will be satisfied by the other if both people follow three norms:

• Mutual Responsiveness. Both people are committed to fulfilling the other's goals and are concerned about the other's well-being.

• Reciprocity. One person's concern for the other results in the other's concern for the first person.

• Equity. The number of times one person gives up his or her interests for the other's benefit should be equal to the number of times the other person gives up his or her needs for the first person's benefit.

Concern for the other person in a conflict may be genuine or instrumental. Genuine concern is based on friendship, love, and collegiality (Clark and Mills 1979). Instrumental concern is based on perceived interdependence: One person has some control over the other's rewards and penalties (D.W. Johnson and R. Johnson 1989). In both cases, the concern is based on a view of the future after the conflict has been resolved. People involved in escalating conflicts often lose awareness of the future and concentrate so hard on winning in the present that they lose track of the importance of maintaining good relationships. The danger of smoothing is that it may be perceived as weakness, thus encouraging the other person to use forcing in future conflicts.

You should not give up your interests and let the other person have what he or she wants because you are afraid. Inappropriate smoothing hides your true interests from the other person. You agree to a course of action that is detrimental to you because you want to be liked or you think that the relationship is too fragile to survive an open conflict. You may be afraid that discussing the conflict may damage the relationship or that if the conflict continues, someone will get hurt, ruining the relationship. You avoid the conflict in favor of superficial harmony.

Compromise When Time Is Short

Compromise is based on the premise that half a loaf is better than none. You are willing to sacrifice part of your goals and part of the relationship to find a quick agreement. Compromise is used when there is not enough time to engage in problem-solving negotiations and both the goal and the relationship seem moderately important. For example, only 20 minutes of computer time are left, and both you and your classmate want to use the computer. Compromising so that each gets the computer for 10 minutes may be the best way to resolve the conflict.

The procedure for compromising is to propose an agreement that usually requires each person to give up 50 percent of what he or she wants so that both of you meet in the middle. Even though compromising appears to be an equal distance from the four other strategies, it lies between problem solving and smoothing and far away from withdrawing and forcing (van de Vliert 1990, van de Vliert and Prein 1989).

The problem with compromising is that any agreement reached may reflect a mechanical splitting of the difference between positions rather than a solution carefully crafted to meet the legitimate interests of each person. The result is frequently an agreement less satisfactory to each person than it could have been. Sometimes, though, you should be satisfied with less. Remember the story of the boy and the nuts. A boy who is very fond of nuts is told one day that he can have a handful.

"As big a handful as I like?" he asks.

"As big a handful as you can take," his mother replies. The boy at once puts his hand into the pitcher of nuts and grasps all his fist can hold. But when he tries to get his hand out, he finds he cannot because the neck of the pitcher is too narrow. He tries and tries to squeeze his hand through. At last he bursts into tears. There he stands crying, yet unwilling to let a single nut go.

"The fault is not with the pitcher," his mother says. "It is your greed that makes you cry. Be satisfied with half as many nuts and you will be able to get your hand out."

Engage in Problem-Solving Negotiations

He that wrestles with us strengthens our nerves and sharpens our skill. Our antagonist is our helper.

—Edmund Burke

When your goals and the relationship are highly important, initiate problem-solving negotiations. The process involves directly expressing your view of the conflict and your feelings about it and inviting the other person to do the same. The aim is to clarify and explore the issues, the nature and strength of the disputants' underlying interests, and the disputants' current feelings. A number of studies have found that such an approach is related to the constructive resolution of conflicts (Burke 1969, 1970; Lawrence and Lorsch 1967).

In considering how to handle a conflict, you need to decide whether to negotiate or stay silent. If you decide to negotiate, the next step is to choose an appropriate time to initiate the process, focusing on the problem, not the person, and taking the easy conflicts first.

To Talk or to Button Your Lips

It is impossible to interact day after day without conflicts arising. When individuals work together, sharing ideas, information, resources, and materials, they are bound to encounter problems. They must decide whether to face a conflict and solve the problem or keep silent and let the conflict continue. An open discussion is not always helpful. Assuming that you can always be open and discuss a conflict with another person is a mistake. Assuming that you can never openly and directly discuss a conflict with another person is also a mistake.

Whether you decide to open your mouth or button your lips depends on the other person and the situation. You should ask yourself two questions:

- "What is my relationship with the other person like?" Generally, the stronger the relationship, the more direct and open your discussion can be.
- "How able is the other person to discuss the conflict?" The other person may not be able to discuss the conflict in a positive way if that person's anxiety or distress level is too high, ability to change is too low, ego or self-esteem is too low, or conflict resolution skills are too low.

Initiate negotiations only if you think the relationship is strong enough and the other person is able to discuss the conflict in a problem-solving, helpful way.

Making a Date: Do Not Hit and Run!

Beginning a discussion of the conflict does not mean that the conflict will be quickly resolved. It is a start, not the end. Be prepared to spend some time in negotiations. You need to time your discussion so that you do not hit and run. A hit-and-run occurs when you start a conversation about the conflict, give your definition and feelings, and then disappear before the other person has a chance to respond. Hit-and-runs tend to be harmful, creating resentment and anger rather than a constructive discussion of the conflict.

Timing is one of the most important elements in initiating negotiations. Discussions are often destructive if they begin when the other person is not in the right frame of mind to face a conflict, perhaps because that person is tired, in a hurry, upset over another problem, or feeling sick. When time is short or the other person cannot commit full attention to the conflict, request to discuss the conflict later. Make an appointment.

Focusing on the Problem, Not the Person

Separating the person from the problem is imperative. Avoid personalized attacks. You should keep the negotiations free of personal criticism, recriminations, abusive language, and especially those subtle jibes that inflict pain. The following suggestions can help you keep the right focus:

• Make it clear that you disagree with ideas and actions, not the other individual as a person.

• Separate the other person's criticism of your actions and ideas from rejection of you as a person.

• Keep your sense of humor.

• Keep all "weapons" out of reach. Do not let one of you hurt the other.

• Protect the other's ego. Provide acceptable reasons for the other person to switch to your viewpoint.

Managing Your Emotions Skillfully

Conflict among individuals in long-term, ongoing relationships tends to breed more intense emotions than conflicts among strangers

(Berscheid 1983; Johnson 1971a, 1971b). Intense emotions also result when people we depend on are unresponsive to our needs (Tjosvold 1977) and take advantage of our concern about their outcomes and the relationship. The most troublesome feelings to deal with are probably anger and fear. You cannot initiate negotiations effectively if you are angry and want to punish or hurt the other person. You cannot initiate negotiations effectively if you are afraid that the other person will lose his or her temper and harm you psychologically or physically. Only when your emotions are under control can you initiate problem-solving negotiations successfully.

Taking Easy Conflicts First

Learn to walk before you run. If you cannot identify a small issue, you may wish to choose a large one and divide it into smaller parts. You can then piece small agreements together into a sizable package. Also, do not wait too long to initiate negotiations. Begin when issues are immediate, small, and concrete—they are easier to negotiate.

Trust

The greater the trust between disputants, the more likely they are to engage in problem-solving negotiations. Trust (and liking) tends to be high in the following situations:

• Disputants expect to engage in future cooperative interaction with each other (D.W. Johnson and S. Johnson 1972, S. Johnson and D.W. Johnson 1972).

• One disputant perceives the other disputant as a member of his or her group (Kramer and Brewer 1984, Yamagishi and Sato 1986).

• Disputants are engaged in a cooperative process that requires the efforts of both to succeed (Deutsch 1962).

• Disputants believe that they or a third party can punish the other for failing to cooperate (Yamagishi 1986).

• Disputants help each other when one believes that the other will reciprocate (Loomis 1959) or when one has recently been helpful or cooperative toward the other (Cooper and Fazio 1979, Kelley and Stahelski 1970). Actions that are seen as voluntary, costly, not a result of situational pressures, and not required by the other's role elicit helpful behavior (Jones and Davis 1965, Komorita 1973).

Use Your Sense of Humor

Humor is essential for keeping conflicts constructive. Keep your sense of humor, and help the other person do the same. Do not make the same mistake as Sam and Sally. Sam and Sally worked as copywriters for different advertising firms. Their job was to think up humorous lines for commercials. One of the things they most enjoyed about each other was their sense of humor. Yet when they began to talk about a conflict, they buried all humor—yelling, screaming, forcing, withdrawing, pouting, and trying to hurt each other. Anger locked away their creativity. Their relationship dramatically improved when they learned to stop yelling and wrote three humorous lines about the nature of a conflict to share with each other.

If laughter is not the best medicine, it is surely one of the best. Any conflict will seem easier to resolve after disputants have laughed about it. Laughter can help keep you healthy not only psychologically but also physically. Laughter is a reflex, a series of involuntary spasms of the diaphragm. This movement forces the breathing muscles to contract and relax in quick succession, increasing the size of the chest cavity—which allows the lungs to take in more oxygen and expel more carbon dioxide than normal. As a result, laughter exercises the lungs, increases the blood's oxygen level, increases circulation and metabolism, and gently tones the entire cardiovascular system—"internal jogging." Muscles of the chest, abdomen, and face get a gentle workout and if the joke is a real winner, so do the arms and legs. Following a laugh, these muscles relax, and pulse rate and blood pressure temporarily decline. Since muscle relaxation and anxiety cannot exist at the same time, a good, hearty laugh may buy you up to 45 minutes of relaxation. Laughter also releases endorphins, the body's natural painkiller.

In following these rules, remember that the most competent business executives, managers, and supervisors generally use problem-solving negotiations and smoothing as their dominant conflict strategies. Such people tend to be highly relationship oriented, problem solving when the goals and needs involved in a conflict are important and smoothing when they are not. Incompetent business administrators use forcing and withdrawing most frequently. In schools, staff typically use forcing and withdrawing the most. When faced with misbehaving students, teachers often first try to force them to behave and then to expel them from the classroom or school (which is a form of withdrawing). Learning how to use all five strategies appropriately so that you can choose how you wish to manage your conflicts empowers you.

Most of the time, you will want to initiate problem-solving negotiations and smoothing, because these are the two strategies that work best in long-term, ongoing relationships. When the goal is important, initiate problem-solving negotiations. When it is not, smooth. You will rarely want to force or withdraw. Compromising is usually only helpful if problem solving has failed or when not enough time is available to resolve the conflict.

The five strategies present a somewhat simplified view of managing conflicts. The complexities of the interaction between two individuals far exceed their initial approaches to a conflict. Conflicts can deteriorate. Initial strategies are usually followed by backup strategies that are followed by other strategies based on what the other person is doing. For example, you may wish to initiate problem solving, but when faced with a colleague who is forcing, you may want to force back. You need to be aware of your backup strategies as well as your dominant one. Your second most frequently used strategy is the one you will tend to use when you are highly anxious and upset.

7

Teaching Students to Negotiate

*Not everything that is faced can be changed but
Nothing can be changed until it is faced.*

—James Baldwin

Negotiation is woven into the daily fabric of our lives in and out of school. Conflicts continually occur, we negotiate resolutions, and we live with the consequences of the agreements we make. We spend a great deal of time negotiating, although we are not always aware we are doing it. Yet many students and faculty do not know how to negotiate, and those who do often negotiate poorly. Negotiating with skill and grace is hard. To resolve conflicts constructively, students must learn how to negotiate.

Teaching students how to negotiate is the first of three stages in conflict resolution/peer mediation training. The second teaches them how to mediate; the third explains how teachers use arbitration if negotiation and mediation fail. Figure 7.1 shows how the training fits into a conflict resolution program.

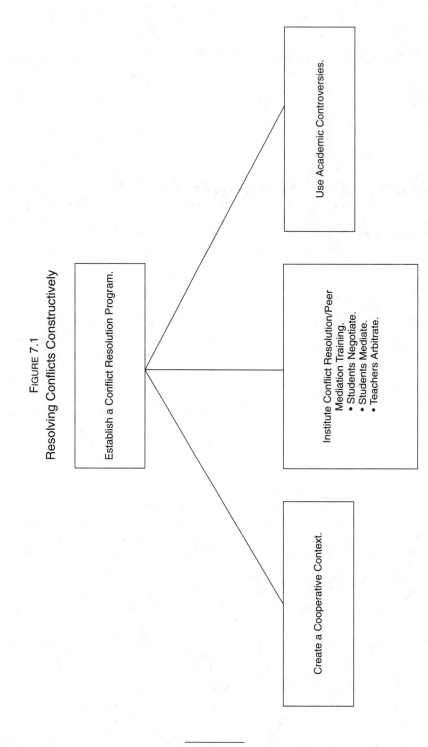

FIGURE 7.1
Resolving Conflicts Constructively

Establish a Conflict Resolution Program.

Use Academic Controversies.

Institute Conflict Resolution/Peer
Mediation Training.
• Students Negotiate.
• Students Mediate.
• Teachers Arbitrate.

Create a Cooperative Context.

Two Types of Negotiating

Negotiation is a process by which persons who have shared and opposed interests want to work out an agreement (D.W. Johnson and F. Johnson 1994). We generally engage in two types of negotiating: One resolves temporary conflicts of interests with strangers, and one resolves ongoing conflicts of interests with family, colleagues, and friends.

Two students, Meg Mine and Nennah Notyours have lost their pencils. In searching the floor, Meg spots a pencil under Nennah's desk and proclaims that she has found her lost pencil.

"Hey," Nennah says, "That's my pencil! I can tell by the teeth marks!"

"Not a chance," replies Meg. "See these scratch marks on the side of the pencil? I always do that with my fingernail!"

Meg and Nennah have a choice as to how they will negotiate for the pencil. They can each try to get the pencil and see who wins, or they can try to find a mutually satisfying solution. Both types of negotiating are appropriate under certain circumstances.

Win-Lose Negotiations

> People . . . are trying to either shun conflict or crush it. Neither strategy is working. Avoidance and force only raise the level of conflict . . . They have become parts of the problem rather than the solution.
>
> —DeCecco and Richards 1974

In win-lose negotiations, you try to make an agreement more favorable to yourself than to the other person. Your goal is important, and the relationship with the other person has no future. You go for a win by making an extreme opening proposal, such as offering $500 for a car when you are willing to pay $1,500. You then compromise slowly, trying to get the other person to compromise first, and pointing out everything that is wrong and unreasonable about the other person's position. You have to be ready to walk away with no agreement.

Assuming that you will never be interdependent with the other person again is often a mistake. And assuming that the conflict cannot be redefined as a mutual problem to be solved is also a mistake. A famous example is the dispute between Israel and Egypt. When Egypt and Israel sat down to negotiate at Camp David in October 1978, an intractable conflict seemed to exist between them. Egypt demanded the immediate return of the entire Sinai Peninsula; Israel, which had occupied the Sinai since the 1967 Middle East war, refused to return an inch of the land. Efforts to reach an agreement, including the proposal of a compromise in which each nation would retain half of the Sinai, proved unacceptable to both sides. As long as the dispute was defined in terms of what percentage of the land each side would control, the two sides could not reach an agreement. Once both realized that what Israel really cared about was the security that the land offered, while Egypt was primarily interested in sovereignty over it, they broke the stalemate. The two countries were then able to reach an integrative solution: Israel would return the Sinai to Egypt in exchange for assurances of a demilitarized zone and Israeli air bases in the Sinai.

The times in your life when you negotiate with someone whom you will never interact with again are rare. Most of the time, therefore, you will want to engage in problem-solving negotiations.

Problem-Solving Negotiations

By blending the breath of the sun and the shade, true harmony comes into the world.

—Tao Te Ching

Imagine that you and another person are rowing a boat across the ocean and you cannot row the boat by yourself. Although the two of you may have conflicts about how to row, how much to row, and what direction to row, you and the other person need food and water to survive. Your conflicts become mutual problems that must be solved to each person's satisfaction. You negotiate to solve a problem because your goals are important to you and you have an ongoing cooperative relationship with the other person that must be maintained in good working order. The aim is to reach an agreement that will benefit everyone involved. Such an agreement is called an integrative solution, and it has many advantages:

• Joins the two parties' interests, thus reducing resistance to reaching an agreement.

• Tends to be highly stable because it maximizes joint benefit. Compromises, coin tosses, and other mechanical agreements are often unsatisfying to one or both parties and therefore create a situation in which the conflict is likely to appear again later (Thomas 1976).

• Strengthens the relationship between parties. Strong relationships help maintain agreements and facilitate the development of integrative solutions in subsequent conflicts.

• Contributes to the welfare of the broader community of which the two parties are members. For example, a school usually benefits as a whole when students, faculty, and staff are able to reconcile their differences creatively.

Problem-solving negotiations have characteristics that distinguish them from other types of conflict management strategies. Recognizing these characteristics will help you in resolving difficulties that may arise as you proceed through the process:

• Interdependence. You cannot negotiate without the consent and participation of the other disputant. Disputants are dependent upon each other to participate in the negotiating process and to reach an agreement.

• Cooperative and Competitive Goals. Desire to reach an agreement and desire to make that agreement as favorable as possible to yourself create a mixed-motive situation. Disputants face a goal dilemma between maximizing their own outcomes and reaching an agreement. The two goals can seriously interfere with each other.

• Primary and Secondary Gains. Negotiations resolve both types of gains. The nature of an agreement determines the primary gain. The secondary gain is determined by factors influencing the effectiveness of the relationship between the disputants, such as the impact of an angry schoolmate on a disputant's quality of life.

• Dilemmas. Disputants depend on each other to provide information on their wants, goals, and interests. Such dependence creates two dilemmas: one of trustworthiness—Can the other person be trusted to tell the truth?; and one of honesty and openness—Will the other person truthfully reveal information about that person's wants, goals, and interests?

• Norms. Disputants develop contractual norms to spell out the ground rules for negotiating and managing the difficulties involved in reaching an agreement. Two common norms are reciprocity and equity: Reciprocity means one disputant should return the same benefit or harm given that person by the other disputant; equity means that benefits received or costs accrued should be equal between disputants.

• Time. Negotiations have a beginning, middle, and end. Strategies and tactics used to initiate negotiations, exchange proposals and information, and precipitate an agreement can be quite different and sometimes contradictory.

• Difficulty. Negotiating is hard. Using the procedures with skill and finesse takes years of practice.

Within ongoing relationships, you are concerned about the other person's interests. Since you are both striving to achieve the same goals, you negotiate so that each can benefit. Cooperators resolve conflicts as partners, not as adversaries. Follow six steps in negotiating a conflict of interests:

1. Describe what each person wants.
2. Describe how each person feels.
3. Exchange reasons for positions.
4. Understand each other's perspective.
5. Invent options for mutual benefit.
6. Reach a wise agreement.

Describe What You Want

If a man does not know to which port he is sailing, no wind is favorable.

—Seneca

Negotiating begins with describing what you want. All people have a right to their wants, needs, and goals (Alberti 1978). Two major mistakes in defining a conflict are to be aggressive by trying to hurt the other person or to be nonassertive by saying nothing, giving up your interests, and keeping your wants to yourself. You should describe what you want to the other person honestly and in a way that respects both you and that person. But the other person has a right to refuse to meet your wants, needs, and goals if they are seen as destructive to that person's interests. People do not have to act against their self-interests to please someone else. After describing what you want, therefore, do not expect the other person to do exactly as you wish. Do not confuse letting others know what you want with demanding that they act as you think they should.

Communicating what you want involves taking ownership of your interests by making clear, descriptive statements:

• Specify your wants, needs, and goals, using such words as *I, me, my,* or *mine.*

• Acknowledge the other person's goals as part of the problem. Explain how the other person's actions are blocking what you want. Describe behaviors you have observed; do not judge, evaluate, or make inferences about the person's motives, personality, or attitude.

• Focus on the long-term cooperative relationship. Most conflicts of interests deal with current problems. Negotiations within a long-term cooperative relationship include discussing how the relationship can be changed so you both can work together better. During such conversations, you will need to make relationship statements, which describe how the two of you are interacting with each other. A good relationship statement indicates clear ownership (uses *I, me, my,* or *mine*) and describes how you see the relationship. An example is, "I think we need to talk about our disagreement yesterday."

You must also listen carefully to the other person. No set of skills is more important for negotiating than being a good listener (Johnson 1972/1993, 1978/1991). Face the person, stay quiet until your turn, think about what the person is saying, and show you understand. The keystone to good listening is paraphrasing—restating, using your words, what the other person says, feels, and means. Paraphrasing improves communication. When you are restating, you cannot judge or evaluate. Restating also gives the other person direct feedback on how well you understand the messages. If you do not fully understand, the other person can add messages until you do. If you are interpreting a message differently from the way it was intended, the other person can clarify it. Paraphrasing indicates that you want to understand what the other person is saying. It shows that you care enough to listen carefully and you take what the other person is saying seriously.

Often, paraphrasing simply restates what the other person has said. At first, you may feel dumb and awkward until you get used to restating. But the other person will be grateful for a chance to clarify or add to the original statement. Paraphrasing becomes harder when it includes feelings as well as ideas. And it is not limited to only the words the sender uses. Nonverbal cues are also important.

Following a paraphrasing rule can help: Before you can reply to a statement, restate what the other person says, feels, and means correctly and to that person's satisfaction. Use a rhythm to your statements: "You said . . . . I say . . . ." First, you say what the other person said ("You said"), then you reply ("I say").

Jointly Defining the Conflict as a Mutual Problem

Two drivers, coming from different directions, are roaring down a one-lane road. Soon they will crash head-on. If the two drivers define the situation as a competition to see who will "chicken out," they will probably crash and die. If they define the situation as a problem to be solved, they may see a solution in which they alternate giving each other the right-of-way. Small and simple conflicts become major and difficult to resolve when they are defined as competitive and win-lose. A win-lose approach will probably escalate the conflict, increase distress, and damage the future relationship. No one loses when disputants sit down to solve a mutual problem. Major and difficult conflicts become resolvable when they are defined as problems to be solved. This approach can increase communication, trust, liking, and cooperation.

Jointly Defining the Conflict as Small and Specific

Fred wants to join a baseball game on the playground.

"You can't play," Ralph shouts. "We already have our teams!"

"You are no longer my friend," Fred shouts back. "You're selfish and mean! I'll never help you with your homework again!"

In defining a conflict, the tendency is to be global and general. Fred is defining the conflict as one of friendship and gratitude. He could just as easily have defined it as one of arriving late or finding a way to make the teams even.

The smaller and more specifically you can define a conflict, the easier it is to resolve. Think small. Defining a conflict as, "She always lies," makes it more difficult to resolve than defining it as, "Her statement was not true." Remember that small is easy, large is hard!

Describe Your Feelings

Many of us in business, especially if we are very sure of our ideas, have hot tempers. My father knew he had to keep the damage from his own temper to a minimum.

—Thomas Watson Jr.
Chairman Emeritus, IBM

Expressing and controlling your feelings is one of the most difficult parts of resolving conflicts. It is also one of the most important (Johnson 1972/1993, D.W. Johnson and R. Johnson 1991). Many conflicts cannot be resolved unless feelings are openly recognized and expressed. For example, if individuals hide or suppress anger, they may make an agreement but they keep their resentment and hostility toward the other person. Their ability to work effectively with the other person and to resolve future conflicts constructively is damaged. The conflict will tend to reoccur regardless of what the agreement is.

Experiencing and sharing feelings also build and maintain close relationships. Feelings provide the cement that holds relationships together, as well as the means for deepening and making them more effective and personal. Feelings that are not recognized and accepted can bias your judgments, create insecurities that hinder a constructive resolution, and reduce your ability to control your behavior.

Because feelings are internal, the primary way other people can accurately know how you are feeling and reacting is for you to tell them. But communicating clearly is difficult. You may be afraid others will exploit your vulnerability, reject you, or laugh at you. The more personal the feelings, the greater the risk you may feel. And expressing feelings is especially hard during a conflict. Conveying anger, hurt, fear, disappointment, and despair requires skill and experience. Hiding your feelings may also confuse or mislead others about how you really feel. For example, you may cry when you do not want to, raise your voice when it is best not to, or even laugh at a time that disturbs others.

Letting others know what you are feeling depends on your ability to recognize, accept, and express your feelings skillfully and constructively. Inability to communicate clearly and directly may lead to using devices that communicate indirectly—and inadequately (Johnson 1972/1993):

- Labels. "You are rude, hostile, and self-centered."
- Commands. "Shut up!"
- Questions. "Are you always this crazy?"
- Accusations. "You do not care about me!"
- Sarcasm. "I'm glad you are early!"
- Approval. "You are wonderful!"
- Disapproval. "You are terrible!"
- Name-Calling. "You are a creep!"

Such methods are common, but they are ineffective because they do not give a clear message to the receiver. Four methods can help describe a feeling directly (Johnson 1972/1993, 1978/1991):

• Name the feeling. "I feel angry." "I feel embarrassed." "I like you."

• Use sensory descriptions that capture how you feel. "I feel stepped on." "I feel like I'm on cloud nine." "I feel like I've just been run over by a truck."

• Report what kind of action the feeling urges you to do. "I feel like hugging you." "I feel like slapping your face." "I feel like walking on your face."

• Use figures of speech. "I feel like a stepped-on toad." "I feel like a pebble on the beach."

A description of a feeling must be personal (uses *I, me, my,* or *mine*) and direct. The following format may help: I feel _____ (name the feeling) when you _____ (name a specific behavior) because _____ (explain how the behavior affects you). An example is, "I feel angry when you break in line ahead of me because I think it isn't fair and I think you ought to wait your turn like everyone else." Expect at least two results. First, you become more aware of what you actually do feel. Explaining feelings to another person often clarifies them to yourself, too. Second, describing your feelings often begins a dialogue that will improve your relationship. Even negative feelings are worth expressing. They signal that something may be going wrong, and by reporting your feelings, you provide information necessary to help you and the other person understand and improve your relationship.

Verbal and nonverbal expression of feelings must be consistent. Many communication difficulties experienced in relationships spring from giving contradictory messages to others by indicating one kind of feeling with words, another with actions, and still another with nonverbal expressions.

Exchange Reasons for Positions

To be persuasive we must be believable; to be believable we must be credible; to be credible, we must be truthful.

—Edward R. Murrow

After you and the other person have described what you both want and feel, listened carefully to each other, and jointly defined the conflict as a small and specific mutual problem, you need to exchange the reasons for your positions. Such a procedure involves the following activities:

• Expressing cooperative intentions.
• Presenting your reasons and listening to the other person's reasons.
• Focusing on wants and interests, not positions.
• Clarifying the differences between your interests and the other person's interests.
• Empowering the other person.

Expressing Cooperative Intentions: Enlarging the Shadow of the Future

Highlighting the long-term, cooperative nature of the relationship is a good way to begin discussing why you and the other person have taken certain positions. Stress that you want to handle the conflict in a cooperative, problem-solving way. You can say, "This situation means that we will have to work together"; "Let's cooperate in reaching an agreement"; or "Let's try to reach an agreement that is good for both of us." State that you are committed to maximizing joint outcomes. Successful negotiation requires finding out what the other person really wants and needs and showing that person how to get it while you get what you want. Enlarge the shadow of the future by affirming that you are committed to the continuation and success of the joint cooperative efforts. Your statement could include the long-term mutual goals and ways the two of you will be interdependent in the future.

Clearly expressing cooperative intentions results in high-quality agreements in a short amount of time. The other person becomes less defensive, more willing to change his or her position, less concerned about who is right and who is wrong, and more understanding of your views and ideas (Johnson 1971a, 1974; D.W. Johnson, McCarty, and

Allen 1976). You are also seen as an understanding and trustworthy person who can be confided in.

Presenting Your Reasons, Listening to the Other Person's Reasons

Saying what you want and how you feel is not enough—you must also give your reasons. For example, "I want to use the computer now, and I'm angry at you for not letting me have it," needs to be followed with, "I have an important homework assignment due today, and this is my only chance to get it done." Your reasons are aimed at informing the other person and persuading that person to agree with you.

You may have to ask more than once why the other person has taken a certain position. For example, you ask a friend to study with you. She replies, "No." Until you understand the reasons for the no, you will not be able to think creatively of ways for both of you to get what you want. The question you can use is, "May I ask why?" If the answer is vague, you add, "Can you be more specific? What do you mean when you say . . . ? I'm not sure I understand." Your tone of voice is as important as the words. If you sound sarcastic, your attempt to understand the other person will backfire.

In listening carefully to the other person's reasons, you must stay flexible, changing your position and feelings when persuaded to do so. Negotiating is a rational process. You are seeking a way to reach your goals, and the other person is doing the same. How successful you are in reaching an agreement depends on how creatively you can think of alternatives that are good for both.

Once each of you has explained your reasons, either may agree or disagree to help reach the other person's goals. The decision to help or to keep negotiating is based on two factors:

- How important your goal is to you.
- How important the other person's goal is to that person.

You must decide whether the other person's reasons are valid. If you think that the other person's goals are more important to that person than yours are to you, then you may wish to agree. Giving up your goals to help the other person reach goals only works if the other person does the same for you 50 percent of the time.

If you think the other person's reasons are not valid, you need to point out the inadequacies of the other person's proposal. If neither you nor the other person is convinced to give up your own goals to fulfill each other's goals, then the two of you must reaffirm your cooperative relationship and explore each other's reasons at a deeper level.

Focusing on Wants and Interests, Not Positions

Susan is usually a compliant student in Mr. Johnson's English class. Today, however, she comes up to Mr. Johnson's desk and states, "I won't do this homework assignment. I don't care what you do to me, I'm not going to do it!" Mr. Johnson, having read this book, immediately recognizes that Susan is presenting a position, and he does not yet know what her underlying needs and wants are.

He says, "May I ask why?" Successful negotiation requires that you approach the other person on the basis of that person's wants and goals.

A classic example showing the need to separate interests from positions is the story of two sisters who each want the only orange available. One sister wants the orange peel to make a cake; the other wants the inner pulp to make orange juice. Their positions—"I want the orange!"—are opposed, but their interests are not. Often, when conflicting parties reveal their underlying interests, finding a solution that suits both is possible.

The heart of negotiating is meeting the goals of the other person while meeting your goals. The success of negotiating depends upon finding out what the other person really wants and showing that person a way to get it while you get what you want. Reconcile wants and goals, not positions. For every want or goal, several possible positions that could satisfy it usually exist. A common mistake is to assume that because the other person's position is opposed to yours, that person's goals are also opposed. Behind opposed positions lie shared and compatible goals, as well as conflicting ones. To identify the other person's wants and goals, ask "Why?" and "Why not?" Think about the person's choice, and realize that the other person has many different wants and goals.

Differentiating Before Integrating

You cannot resolve a conflict until you know what you are disagreeing about. You must understand the differences between your wants and needs and those of the other person. The more you differentiate between your interests and those of the other person, the better you will be able to integrate them into a mutually satisfying agreement. In discussing a conflict, try to find the answers to these questions: "What are the differences between my wants and needs and yours?" "Where are our needs and goals the same?" "What actions of the other person do I find unacceptable?" "What actions of mine does the other person find unacceptable?"

Empowering the Other Person

Shared power and wise agreements go hand in hand. One way to empower the other person is by making sure you are open to negotiations and flexible about the option you like the best. If that person can negotiate with you, then he or she has power and options. Willingness to negotiate means you are open to the possibility that a better option than you now realize may be available. You do not want to become overcommitted to any one position until an agreement is reached. Another way to empower the other person is to provide choice among options. Generate a variety of possible solutions before deciding what to do. For example, if Susan says to Mr. Johnson, "You have to agree to let me not do my homework!" he will feel powerless. If Susan says, "Let's think of three possible agreements, and then choose the one that seems the best!" both she and Mr. Johnson feel powerful.

The psychological costs of feeling helpless to resolve grievances include frustration, anxiety, and friction. When a person feels powerless, that person may become hostile and try to tear down the system, or apathetic and throw in the towel. Neither reaction is productive. We all need to believe that we have been granted a fair hearing and that we have the power and the right to gain justice when we have been wronged.

Potential Problems

• People do not always understand the interests underlying their position and therefore cannot describe them to others.

• Disputants may not wish to reveal their interests because they are afraid that the other will use the information to personal advantage. Disclosing your wants, goals, and interests always carries the risk that the other person may exploit your vulnerability.

• A person's interests are often organized into hierarchical trees. The initial interests, which are the ones discussed, are the tip of the iceberg. More discussion may reveal deeper interests.

Understand Each Other's Perspective

The test of a first-rate intelligence is the ability to hold two opposed ideas in the mind at the same time, and still retain the ability to function.

—F. Scott Fitzgerald

To negotiate successfully, you must be able to take the other person's perspective and understand how the conflict appears to that person. Perspective-taking is the ability to comprehend how a situation appears to another person and how that person is reacting cognitively and emotionally to the situation. The opposite of perspective-taking is egocentrism, the inability to recognize that other perspectives exist and that one's view of the conflict is incomplete and limited.

Juanita and Betsy sit by each other in class. Juanita comes from an upper middle-class family. Betsy's parents struggle to pay the rent and provide enough food for the family. Betsy and Juanita both win $20 in a school drawing.

Juanita says, "Hey, I won $20. Imagine that." Then she continues eating lunch and reading a magazine.

Betsy starts jumping up and down shouting, "I won! I won! I won $20!" She throws her arms around her friend, crying and laughing in her excitement. Why did Juanita and Betsy react so differently to the news that they had each won $20 in a school drawing?

Different people have different perspectives, which developed from responding to their life experiences. No two people see an issue in exactly the same way; each interprets identical events differently. A person's perspective selects and organizes what the person addresses and experiences. In other words, people generally see only what their perspective allows them to see. For example, a rich person and a poor person may see a homeless person differently because they have different perspectives.

People are influenced not only by their perspective but also by their focus: They tend to only see what they want to see. Out of a mass of detailed information, people focus on those facts that confirm their prior perceptions and disregard or misinterpret those that call their perceptions into question. Each side in a negotiation usually sees only the merits of its case and only the faults of the other side.

A person can have different perspectives at different times. For example, if you have been lifting 100-pound bags of cement and someone tosses you a 40-pound bag, it will seem very light. But if you have been lifting 20-pound bags, the 40-pound bag will seem quite heavy. When you are hungry, you notice all the food in a room. When you are not hungry, the food does not attract your attention. Your perspective changes as your life changes.

The same message can have two meanings from two different perspectives. For example, if you provoke your coworker, she may laugh. But if you provoke your boss, she may get angry and fire you! One perspective interpreted the message as friendly teasing; the other, as hostile insubordination. A person's perspective determines how a message will be interpreted.

Understanding logically how the other person views a problem is not enough—you also need to empathize with the other's point of view and feel the emotional force with which that person believes in it. You may see on the table a glass half full of water. The other person may see a dirty, half-empty glass about to cause a ring on a mahogany finish. Change a person's perspective, and you change what the person addresses and the way the person interprets the events in his or her life. Understand the other's perspective, and you improve your ability to find integrative solutions to the conflict.

Misunderstandings often occur when we assume that everyone sees things from the same perspective that we do. If you like Italian food, you assume that all your friends like Italian food. If you are interested in sports, you assume that everyone is interested in sports. If you think a teacher is stupid, you are surprised when a peer thinks the teacher is brilliant.

Failing to understand the other's perspective increases the possibility that the conflict will be managed destructively. In their study of conflict in schools, DeCecco and Richards (1974) found that an inability to take the perspectives of others impeded negotiations as a means of conflict resolution. Failure of teachers and administrators to perceive correctly the interests of students resulted in destructive procedures for managing conflicts.

Negotiators often misunderstand and distort the positions of disputants because of poor communication. Perspective-taking improves communication and reduces misunderstandings by influencing how messages are phrased and received. The better you understand the other person's perspective, the better you can phrase messages so the other person can understand them. For example, if a person does not know what snow is, you would not refer to "corn snow" or "fresh powder." Understanding the other person's perspective also helps you accurately understand the messages you are receiving from that person. For example, if the other person says, "That's just great!" the meaning reverses if you know the person is frustrated.

Perspective-taking improves the relationship with the other person. You are more liked and respected when the other person realizes that you are seeing his or her perspective accurately and using it to create potential agreements that benefit both sides equally.

To reach a wise agreement, you must clearly understand the common and opposed interests in a conflict; accurately assess their validity and relative merits; and think creatively to propose workable solutions. Such actions require that you see a conflict from both your own and the other person's perspective and keep both perspectives in mind at the same time. You can check to see if you accurately understand the situation from the other person's perspective by asking for clarification, known as perception checking; paraphrasing; and presenting the other person's position from that person's perspective.

Checking Your Perception

Before you respond to a person's feelings, you need to make sure you know what the other person actually feels. When people describe their feelings, we can usually accept that what they say is accurate. But if people express their feelings indirectly (e.g., through sarcasm) or nonverbally (e.g., through a frown), we often need to clarify how they feel. A perception check is the best way to ensure that you understand how a person feels:

- Describe what you think the other person's feelings are.
- Ask whether your perception is accurate.
- Refrain from expressing approval or disapproval of the feelings.

"You look sad. Are you?" is an example of a perception check. It describes how you think the person is feeling; it asks the person to agree with or correct your perception; and it does not make a value judgment about the feeling. A perception check communicates the message, "I want to understand your feeling—is this the way you feel?" It invites people to describe their feelings more directly. And it shows you care enough about the person to want to understand how the person feels.

Perception checking will help you avoid actions you may later regret—actions that were based on false assumptions. Our impressions are often biased by our own fears, expectations, and present feelings. For example, if we are afraid of anger and expect others to be angry, then we may think they will reject us.

Paraphrasing

You must not only understand the other person's perspective, you must also let the person know that you understand. Paraphrasing helps you get into the other person's shoes and see the conflict from the other point of view. When you state in your words what the other person says, feels, and means, you not only avoid judging, but also provide feedback on how well you understand the other person's position.

Presenting the Other Person's Position

Role-play helps you gain insight into the other person's perspective. You role-play that you are the other person and present that person's position and reasoning. Then the other person role-plays your position and reasoning. The more involved the two of you get in arguing for the other's position, the more you will understand how the conflict appears from the other person's viewpoint. This type of role-play is called role reversal, and the procedure is discussed in Chapter 8.

Role-play is invaluable in finding solutions that are mutually acceptable. A series of studies on the impact of perspective reversal on the resolution of conflicts (Johnson 1971) indicates that skillful role reversal increases cooperative behavior between negotiators, clarifies misunderstanding of the other's position, increases understanding of the other's position, and aids one's ability to perceive the issue from the other's frame of reference. Johnson found that role reversal can result in a reevaluation of the issue and a change of attitude toward it. The role reverser is perceived as a person who is generally understanding, cooperative, and trustworthy.

Invent Options for Mutual Gain

One completely overcomes only what one assimilates.

—Andre Gide

People generally agree to the first reasonable solution proposed. But such action shuts off considering what may be more advantageous agreements. Make sure you generate at least three good alternative agreements before deciding which one to adopt. Knowing some obstacles to avoid and ways to think creatively can help in this process.

Avoiding Obstacles

Inventing options does not come naturally. Not inventing options is the normal state of affairs, even within the easiest negotiations. Try not to let the following obstacles inhibit you:

• Judging prematurely. A critical attitude waiting to pounce on the drawbacks of any new idea is the primary impediment to creative thinking.

• Searching for the single answer. Premature closure and fixation on the first proposal offered as the single best answer short-circuits wise decision making.

• Assuming a fixed pie. Do not assume that the less for you, the more for the other person. Expand the pie. For example, suppose you want to see one movie and your date wants to see another. You also know your date likes to eat at a certain restaurant. By enlarging the pie to include which restaurant you go to for dinner before going to a movie, an integrative agreement is possible (one picks the restaurant, the other picks the movie).

• Focusing on your own immediate needs and goals. To meet your needs in an ongoing relationship, you also have to meet the other person's needs. Shortsighted self-concern leads to partisan positions, partisan arguments, and one-sided solutions.

• Sticking with the status quo to avoid fear of the unknown. Changing can create anxiety about potential new and unknown problems and guilt over past ineffective or inappropriate behavior. People often try to justify their actions by refusing to change.

Creative Options

Follet (1973) gives an example of how two people in a conflict created a workable option. They are reading in a library room. One wants to open the window for ventilation, the other to keep it closed in order not to catch cold. To resolve their conflict, they search for creative options. They finally agree to open a window in the next room, thereby letting in fresh air while avoiding a draft. Potential agreements that maximize joint outcomes often take creative problem solving. The following suggestions can stimulate creative thinking:

• Think of as many options as possible. The more options you have, the greater the room for negotiations.

• Separate inventing options from judging them. Invent first, judge later.

• Gather as much information as possible about the problem. The more you know, the easier you can find solutions.

• See the problem from different perspectives and reformulate it to let new orientations emerge. Such a reformulation often produces insight that is exciting and leads to new solutions.

• Search for mutual gains. Try to maximize joint outcomes.

• Invent ways of making decisions easily. Give the other person choices that are as painless as possible. If you want a horse to jump a fence, you do not raise the fence. Propose "yesable" agreements.

• Test each proposed agreement against reality. What are its strengths and weaknesses? What does each person gain and lose? How does it maximize joint outcomes?

Different types of agreements can help maximize joint outcomes:

◊ Expanding the Pie. Find ways to increase the resources available. Many conflicts arise from a perceived resource shortage.

◊ Package Deals. Incorporate several related issues into one agreement. For example, a package deal that includes completing homework, improving classroom behavior, and helping another student may be easier to negotiate together rather than separately.

◊ Trade-Offs. Exchange two different things of comparable value. For example, a student may agree to do her homework if the teacher agrees to never call on her in class.

◊ Tie-Ins. An issue that the other person considers extraneous is introduced. You offer to accept a certain settlement if this issue is settled to your satisfaction.

◊ Carve-Outs. Carve an issue out of a larger context, leaving the related issues unsettled.

◊ Logrolling. Both people give up their low-priority issues that are high priority to the other person.

◊ Cost Cutting. One person gets what that person wants, and the other's cost of conceding on those issues is reduced or eliminated.

◊ Bridging. Create a new option that satisfies both people's interests and that is different from what each originally thought they wanted. For example, Rubin, Pruitt, and Kim (1994) present a married couple in conflict over whether to vacation at the seashore or in the mountains. After some discussion, they identify their interests as swimming and fishing. They then agree to visit a lake region that is neither at the seashore nor in the mountains, but offers excellent swimming and fishing.

When you invent alternative agreements, describe what you are doing and neglecting to do that may be creating and continuing the conflict. Neglecting to carry out a constructive action may create and continue the conflict as much as carrying out a destructive action. You may need to change your actions. Even though you may want the other person to change, you can change your actions easier than you can change those of the other person! It would be nice if everyone else changed so we would never have to. But you do not have control over the actions of others—only your own.

After inventing a number of options, you and the other person will have to agree on which one to try out first. Remember Aesop's fable about the mice in trouble:

The mice are saying, "It's terrible! Just terrible! We really must do something about it! But what?" The mice are talking about the cat. One by one, they are falling into her claws. She would steal up softly, then spring suddenly, and there would be one mouse less. The mice finally hold a meeting to decide what to do. After some discussion a young mouse jumps up.

"I know what we should do!" he exclaims. "Tie a bell around the cat's neck! Then we will hear her coming and we can run away fast!"

The mice joyfully clap their paws. What a good idea! Why hadn't they thought of it before? And what a very clever little fellow this young mouse is!

But now a very old mouse, who hadn't opened her mouth during the whole meeting, gets up to speak. "Friends, I agree that the plan of the young mouse is very clever indeed. But I should like to ask one question. Which of us is going to tie the bell around the cat's neck?"

The moral is, adopting an option that cannot be implemented by one or both people is useless.

Reach a Wise Agreement

I never let the sun set on a disagreement with anybody who means a lot to me.

—Thomas Watson Sr.
Founder, IBM

Given that we are all separate individuals with our own unique wants and needs, whenever we interact with others, we will have some interests that are congruent and others that are in conflict. A wise agreement manages the combination of shared and opposed interests by meeting certain criteria:

• The agreement must meet the legitimate needs of all participants and be viewed as fair by everyone involved. In deciding which option to adopt, keep in mind the importance of preserving good feelings, mutual interests, and shared history. Focus on the long-term relationship by pointing out that no agreement should jeopardize it or either person's happiness. The agreement should specify the responsibilities and rights of everyone involved in implementing it. Ensure that you include the following elements:

◊ How each person will act differently in the future. These responsibilities should be specific, telling who does what, when, where, and how; realistic, ensuring that each can do what he or she is agreeing to do; and shared, obtaining agreement that each person will do a different job.

◊ How the agreement will be reviewed and renegotiated if it turns out to be unworkable. Indicate ways that cooperation will be restored if one person slips and acts inappropriately. Decide when participants will meet to discuss whether the agreement is working and what further steps can be taken to improve cooperation. You cannot be sure the agreement will work until you try it out. After you have tested it for a while, set aside some time to talk over how things are going. You may find that you need to make some changes or even rethink the conflict. Keep on top of it so that the two of you may creatively solve it.

• The agreement must be based on objective criteria (Fisher and Ury 1981). Evaluate each option, using at least one of the following criteria:

◊ Equal chance of benefiting, such as flipping a coin or letting a third-party arbitrator decide.

◊ Fairness, such as taking turns, sharing, and equal use. One way of assessing fairness is to list the gains and losses for each person if the agreement is adopted, and then see if they balance.

◊ Scientific Merit. The agreement is based on theory that has been tested, and evidence indicates it will work.

◊ Community Values. Those who are most in need are taken care of first.

• The process of reaching the agreement and the agreement itself must strengthen participants' ability to work together cooperatively. Participants must remain moral, caring, and just and believe that the other is entitled to caring and justice.

• The process of reaching the agreement and the agreement itself must strengthen participants' ability to resolve future conflicts constructively. Conflicts of interests will reoccur frequently, and each time one is faced and resolved, the procedures and skills used should be strengthened and validated.

Both you and the other person need to be aware of what actions trigger anger and resentment in the other. Criticism, put-downs, sarcasm, and belittling often trigger a conflict. If the two of you understand what not to do as well as what to do, you will be able to resolve the conflict more easily.

Try, Try Again

Difference of opinion leads to inquiry, and inquiry to truth.
—Thomas Jefferson

When you fail at negotiating an integrative agreement, the next step is to start over. To be successful, you must remember to try, try again. No matter how far apart the two sides seem, no matter how opposed your interests seem to be, keep talking. Persistent discussion will eventually produce a viable and wise decision.

When two young students cannot agree, a teacher or administrator may send them to the "problem-solving rug" to keep negotiating until they reach an agreement. Simple rules guide the process:

- Students must sit on the rug until the conflict is resolved.
- Students may not touch—only talking is allowed.
- Be patient. It may take them a long time.
- Students tell the teacher or administrator when they reach an agreement.
- Adult praises them.

Negotiate in Good Faith

You can bring your credibility down in a second. It takes a million acts to build it up, but one act can bring it down . . . . People are suspicious because for several thousand years that suspicion was warranted . . . we try very hard not to do things that will create distrust.

—Howard K. Sperlich
President, Chrysler Corporation

Everyone has a negotiating reputation. You can believe some people's promises; other people rarely keep their commitments. You want to build a reputation as someone who is honest, truthful, trustworthy, and therefore, fulfills promises. You want your word to be good. When your word has not been good in the past, you can use some strategies to repair your reputation:

- Pay your debts. Do whatever you agreed to do in the past but have not yet done. Once you have fulfilled past promises, your current promise will be more credible.
- Use collateral. The collateral should be something of value, something the other person does not expect you to give up. But do not make it so outrageous that it is not believable. For example, promising to give someone $1,000 if you break your word is not believable.
- Ask a cosigner to guarantee your word. Find someone who trusts you and whom the other person also trusts.

Refusal Skills

Not all issues are negotiable. Students need to know when an issue is or is not negotiable and be able to say "no" or "I refuse to negotiate this issue."

Figure 7.2 shows clear and unclear reasons for not negotiating. You will save time and trouble by not trying to persuade others to make agreements they do not wish to make and by not letting others persuade you to agree to something you do not wish to do.

FIGURE 7.2

Reasons for Saying "No" to a Suggested Agreement

Clear	Unclear
It is illegal.	My intuition tells me "no."
It is inappropriate.	I am not sure.
It will hurt other people.	The right option is not there.
I will not be able to keep my word.	I have changed my mind.

8

Mediating Conflicts Among Students

To introduce mediation, educator William Ury often tells a tale of an old gentleman who requested in his will that his estate be divided among his three sons: one-half to his oldest son, one-third to his middle son, and one-ninth to his youngest son. When the loving father dies, his estate consists of 17 camels. The three sons attempt to divide the estate according to their father's wishes but quickly find that they cannot unless they cut some camels into pieces. They argue and argue about how to divide the camels. Eventually, a village elder rides up on her dusty camel and inquires about their problem. The three brothers explain the situation. The elder then offers to make her camel available if that will help. It does. With 18 camels, the brothers can solve the problem. The oldest son takes 9 camels (one-half of 18), the middle son chooses 6 more (one-third of 18), and the youngest son acquires 2 camels (one-ninth of 18). Almost before the three brothers know what has happened, the wise woman climbs back onto her camel and rides off into the setting desert sun.

This story illustrates what a creative mediator can do. Mediators are neutral people who help others resolve a conflict by assisting them through the negotiating process to reach an agreement that participants believe is fair and workable. Mediators do not tell disputants what to do, decide who is right or wrong, or discuss what they would do in such a situation. Mediators are facilitators, with no formal power over disputants.

Mediation is an extension of the negotiating process, using specific strategies to promote efficient and effective negotiations. Successful mediation produces three results:

- The conflict is resolved so that all disputants benefit.
- The relationship between disputants is as good as or better than before the conflict.
- Disputants' negotiating skills and self-confidence in using them increases.

Students can learn to be peer mediators to help classmates negotiate their conflicts. The teacher selects two students each day to be the class mediators. Conflicts that students cannot resolve are referred to the mediators. The role of class mediator is rotated throughout the class so that each student serves an equal amount of time.

Peer mediators have two responsibilities: help students resolve their conflict constructively and teach them how to negotiate effectively. Because student disputes often involve private information, peer mediators must be trusted by their classmates not to tell other students what occurs during mediation sessions. Peer mediators report information to their teacher, however, if they believe that a student is in danger or is committing illegal acts.

Peer mediation is satisfying work. Students not only help their classmates but also learn about others and themselves. Students are not mediators because they are better persons than their classmates. They are mediators because they have been trained in the procedures and skills required, and it is their turn to fulfill the mediator role. At any time, they, too, may need help in resolving a conflict.

To be an effective mediator requires effort and considerable practice. Mediators must know exactly what they are doing and why they are doing it. Figure 8.1 shows general guidelines. A series of steps guide mediators through the process:

1. End hostilities.
2. Ensure that both students are committed to the mediation process.
3. Help students negotiate successfully with each other.
4. Formalize the agreement.

FIGURE 8.1

Mediator Guidelines

Listen closely. Remember that you cannot listen and talk at the same time.

Find out the facts. Ask what happened and what must be done to resolve the conflict.

Analyze what you hear to see if agreement is possible. Think about what students are saying so that you can help them separate their interests from their positions and think of creative solutions to their problem.

Enforce the rules. Do not allow interruptions, insults, or shouting.

Be patient.

Respect both students. Showing respect encourages effective participation.

End Hostilities

Mediation begins with ending hostilities and cooling students down enough so that constructive negotiating can take place. Cooling off does not resolve the conflict—it lowers the emotional level and postpones resolution. Occasionally, students want to skip mediation after they have cooled off. If no hard feelings remain, let them do so. Usually, however, cooling off is a preliminary step to mediating.

Breaking up Fights

Peer mediators are helpers, not police officers—they should find an adult to break up fighting, especially physical fighting. Sometimes a teacher's presence is enough to stop hostilities. Ideally, two teachers should work together. If a teacher (or pair of teachers) intends to separate two students who are physically fighting, the teacher should have a clear (hopefully practiced) plan in mind. Procedures include firmly ordering the students to stop or restraining them. Teachers should never restrain one student without restraining the other, however, because the restrained one will be open to attack from the other. (Such a situation does not win the teacher any points as a peacemaker either.) Restraining fighters should be used only in an emergency; such action may cause students to turn on the teacher.

Another way to end hostilities is to train students to be spectators. Classes learn procedures to stop hostilities and practice them in "fight drills." Tactics include everyone leaving (taking away the audience); surrounding the disputants and chanting, "Stop fighting, stop fighting"; and surrounding them and singing a happy song, such as "Ring Around the Rosy," to create a situation in which fighting is incongruous.

When no adult is available and the class as a whole is not ending the conflict, peer mediators can distract disputants to divert their attention and physical and emotional energy. For example, breaking eye contact between disputants will often stop a fight. A peer mediator can get very close and shout loudly. A more powerful distraction is to reach down by the disputants, pretend to pick up a $10 bill, which was already in the mediator's hand, and loudly say, "Hey, who dropped this $10 bill?" If disputants look to see if the $10 is theirs, then the fight is interrupted and can be ended.

Cooling off Hostile Students

Separating students often helps dissipate their emotions. Classes can practice the following methods for cooling down hostile individuals:

• Cool-off corners. When students have cooled off, they can leave the corners.

• Deep-breathing and muscle relaxation.

1. Take slow, deep breaths while counting to 10 and then back to 1 again.

2. Tense all muscles and breathe in. Keeping muscles tense, hold breath for five seconds. Then slowly exhale and relax muscles for five seconds. Repeat this process several times.

3. When students become skilled in deep breathing and muscle relaxation, teachers ask them to imagine their anger leaking out of their toes as they relax. Their anger drains away through their feet. Then they walk away from it.

• Exhausting physical activities, such as jogging or walking several miles, multiple push-ups, or hitting a punching bag.

• Conflict forms. Mediation is often helped when students reflect on a conflict, define it, and think of alternative ways of resolving it before mediation begins. A conflict form (see Figure 8.2) gathers this information in writing. Each disputant fills out a form. If a student cannot read or write well, the mediator provides a partner to help. After each disputant finishes the form, the mediator reads over the answers with the student and helps with those that the student is unsure of. The mediator then begins mediation, using the conflict form to help disputants communicate their views of the conflict to each other. Students may either talk, or they may exchange the forms and write their reactions to each other's accounts. The mediator also discusses what the students will do in a future similar situation. For each suggestion, the mediator should ask, "Will this action solve the problem better than open hostilities, such as fighting?"

Conflict forms give the mediator and disputants a clear idea of how to proceed. The forms should highlight the cooperation and negotiation procedures and skills the students need to learn to get along better with classmates.

FIGURE 8.2
Gathering Information for Mediation

Conflict Form

1. Who was your conflict with?

2. What did you want?
    a. How did the other person's actions stop you from getting what you want?
    b. How did you feel?

3. What did the other person want?
    a. How did your actions stop that person from getting what was wanted?
    b. How did the other person feel?

4. What are three potential agreements that might resolve the conflict and reestablish a good relationship between the two of you?
    a.
    b.
    c.

5. What are three things you might try if this conflict happens again?
    a.
    b.
    c.

6. Do you have anything you would like to say to the person you had the conflict with? If so, please add here.

Ensure Commitment to Mediation

Once hostilities have stopped and the students have cooled down emotionally, the mediation session can begin. Mediation is the students' choice. If they decide to accept help from the mediator, they must commit themselves to the mediation process and agree to work hard to solve the problem.

The Mediation Area

The arrangement of a mediation area sends a message about whether the mediation will be fair. Before mediation begins, the mediator makes sure the area is neat and clean, arranges the chairs so that the mediator sits at the end of a table and the disputants sit across from one another, and places paper and a pencil on the table for each person. When the mediator is ready, the disputants may enter the area or room.

Introducing the Mediator and the Mediation Process

The mediator must confirm that the disputants understand the mediation process and have committed themselves to making it succeed. A memorized introduction works best. Younger students may need a simpler explanation than older students. The introduction should include the following points, with mediators developing a personal version they are comfortable using:

• Introduce yourself and confirm the disputants' names, making sure they are spelled correctly.

• Explain that you will not take sides or attempt to decide who is right or wrong. The mediator does not tell disputants what to do. The disputants themselves must decide on the solution by negotiating a wise agreement with each other. The mediator has no biases regarding the dispute and will be fair to both sides. The mediator's role is to hear both sides, facilitate the steps of negotiation, help disputants overcome any blocks to a settlement, and help find a solution to their conflict that satisfies both parties.

• Go over the ground rules for mediation and elicit disputants' promise to abide by them (see Figure 8.3).

• Ask if disputants have any questions about mediation.

FIGURE 8.3
Ground Rules for Mediating

Agree to solve the problem. The mediator asks the students if they wish to solve their problem with the mediator's help. Mediation does not proceed until both students say "yes," acknowledging publicly that a conflict exists and they will participate in mediation. Disputants must understand that mediation is voluntary, and no one can force them to participate.

Do not use name-calling. Disputants must be respectful and considerate. Good manners are a necessity.

Do not interrupt. Each person will have an opportunity to state his or her views of the conflict without interruption. While one student is talking, the other disputant should not interrupt or comment.

Act honestly. Negotiations depend on disputants stating honestly and accurately what they want, how they feel, and what their underlying interests are.

Agree to abide by the agreement. Disputants must do what they agree to do.

Maintain confidentiality. Everything that is said is confidential except for information on drugs, weapons, and alcohol on school property or at school events. In these cases, the mediator is required to report it to school authorities.

Assist Negotiations

With the mediator's help, students begin the problem-solving steps in the negotiation process:

1. Describe what happened and what they want.
2. Describe how they feel.
3. Give the reasons for their wants and feelings.
4. Present their understanding of the other's perspective, wants, feelings, and rationale.
5. Develop three optional agreements that maximize joint outcomes.
6. Select one option and reach an agreement.

Helping Students Communicate

The mediator decides who will talk first to relate the facts and events that created and continued the conflict. But before that discussion begins, the mediator should emphasize the cooperative nature of the relationship. Disputants need to recognize their common interests and the importance of maintaining a constructive long-term relationship with each other. They must believe that the future of the relationship is more important than any short-term advantage from winning.

When the wants of one person conflict with those of another, cooperative and competitive interests are present. People can act cooperatively to maximize joint gain, or they can act competitively and work to maximize their own gain at the other person's expense. They can concentrate on cooperative interests:

• We need each other to reach an agreement. If we do not cooperate and solve this problem, neither one of us will get what we want.

• We will work together in the future. If our relationship is damaged, we will have future difficulties that will be worse than not getting what we want today.

Or they can focus on competitive interests:

• We will work toward getting more of the desired resources than the other person gets.

• We are concerned with short-term benefits and a desire to be better off than the other person.

The mediator focuses on cooperative interests by highlighting common ones that disputants share and by describing opposing interests as a mutual problem to be solved rather than as a win-lose situation. Pointing out ways that disputants share a mutual fate and depend on each other for resources and assistance also emphasizes the need for cooperation. Explaining how disputants will lose if they become enemies is another technique.

A potential cost of not resolving the conflict is teacher arbitration, also known as outside enemy interdependence. If students do not resolve the conflict, then the teacher or the principal may decide in a "winner-take-all" fashion. The likelihood of an outcome that satisfies each side is greater through mediation than through arbitration. Reminding students of this advantage may encourage them to negotiate harder.

What Happened

Students may refuse to talk calmly to each other, yelling or accusing instead. At this point, the mediator's role is to ask each disputant to describe what happened, what the disputant wants, and how the disputant feels. The mediator begins by saying, "Tell me what happened." Each student states the facts as calmly as possible. If the nature of the conflict and the events that triggered it are not clear, the mediator helps students figure out what happened by asking questions:

- "Tell me more about . . . ."
- "How long has this been going on?"
- "When did this happen?"
- "What would you like to see happen now?"

What They Want

The mediator says, "Tell the other person what you want." By describing their wants and goals, students define their positions. Many times, students will not fully understand what the problem is. Filling out the conflict form before mediation begins helps, but further clarification may also be necessary. Sometimes stating what each person wants to keep the other from getting, as well as what each one wants for himself or herself, clarifies the problem.

The mediator helps disputants describe what they want without making the other person angry, defensive, or upset. Students should not sabotage their chances for agreement by alienating the other person. Enforcing the no-interruption rule is the mediator's responsibility. As disputants explain what happened and what they want, the mediator's body language should show interest in what each student is saying. The mediator makes eye contact, sits attentively, and listens carefully to understand what issues have to be resolved so that an agreement can be reached. If students cannot give a factual and calm account of the conflict, the mediator may ask them to describe the conflict as if they were a neutral, third-party observer. This change in narrative from first person to third person may provide enough distance for the students to analyze the situation and their behavior without feeling threatened. Mediators also need to make sure the conflict is defined as a small and specific mutual problem that can be solved.

How They Feel

Disputants frequently do not know how they feel. The mediator helps them, without making negative remarks about the other person. Such help includes encouraging them to take ownership of their feelings by using "I" messages and to describe how they feel by naming the feeling or using sensory descriptions (e.g., "I feel stepped on"), actions urges (e.g.,"I want to bury my head in the sand and play ostrich"), or figures of speech (e.g., "I feel as small as an ant"). Often the disputants are angry and frustrated because negotiating has already failed. Consequently, their descriptions may include angry statements. The mediator may have to remind them that no name-calling is allowed.

Avoiding Pressure to Take Sides

Students often demand that the mediator agree that one person is right and the other person is wrong. Remaining neutral and not taking sides is an important mediator skill. The mediator may need to remind disputants that mediators cannot agree or disagree with a person. Certain words and phrases show impartiality and a nonjudgmental tone. For example, rather than saying, "She is angry because you stole her purse," the mediator can say, "She is angry because you had her purse." Rather than saying, "The two of you were yelling at each other about the $15," the mediator can say, "You talk to each other in unhelpful ways when the topic of the money comes up."

Paraphrasing

Paraphrasing helps mediators clarify students' views of the problem and their feelings about it. The mediator must be able to listen attentively and summarize accurately, using the following techniques (Johnson 1972/1993):

• Restate the facts and summarize the events. Follow paraphrasing rules: Put yourself in the other person's shoes; state the other person's ideas and feelings in your own words; use "you" to begin your statements (e.g., "You want," "You feel," and "You think"); and show understanding and acceptance by nonverbal behaviors, such as tone of voice, facial expressions, gestures, eye contact, and posture.

• Reflect feelings. Pay attention to the emotional element in each person's position. Use the statement, "You feel _____ (name the feeling) because _____ (explain why)."

• Remain neutral.

• Refuse to give advice or suggestions. Disputants often ask, "What do you think we should do?" Generally, disputants resist agreements that are imposed on them and support agreements that they develop themselves.

• Avoid bringing up feelings and problems from your own experience. The mediator may have faced conflicts similar to those that disputants now face. The temptation is to say, "Here is what I did when I faced this problem" or "Here is how I felt when that happened to me." Such statements do not help. The mediator is there to help disputants clarify their own goals and feelings, not to make disputants listen to how others dealt with similar situations.

In the following example, a mediator is helping two students, Jeremy and Mark, resolve a conflict about working jointly on a report. Each student states his view of the conflict, and the mediator paraphrases the views to help accurately identify each person's position.

Jeremy: I went to the library to get a book I needed to do the assignment. Mark jumped in front of me and grabbed the book just as I was about to take it off the shelf! It really makes me mad!

Mediator: You are angry and frustrated because Mark took the book you needed just as you were reaching for it.

Jeremy: Right. The only reason that he knew about the book was because I told him about it.

Mediator: You want Mark to give you the book.

Jeremy: Yeah. I want to use it over the weekend.

Mark: I knew about the book long before Jeremy found out about it. I've used it before; that's how I knew where it was. I knew that once Jeremy got it, he would never share, so I had to get it first. He can use it after I'm done.

Mediator: You are feeling hurt. You believe you knew about the book first. You are afraid that if Jeremy checked the book out, you would never get to use it.

Mark: Yeah. Jeremy keeps things at home and does not share them.

Mediator: I'm beginning to understand. Both of you need to use the book. Mark wants to use the book right now. Jeremy wants to take the book home and use it over the weekend. Jeremy is frustrated and angry. Mark, you are hurt and anxious. Right now you are trying to use the book in ways that keep the other person from using it. So far, you have not discussed how to use the book together or share it. Does that sound right?

Jeremy and Mark: Yes.

Mediator: We can start thinking of optional solutions now.

Research shows that paraphrasing is an essential skill for mediators (Johnson 1972/1993, 1978/1991):

• Makes students feel understood and supported. Defensiveness may decrease, allowing students to think of new ways to resolve the conflict.

• Clarifies students' wants, goals, and feelings. By restating what disputants have said, the mediator provides an opportunity for them to affirm or correct the mediator's understanding.

• Helps students listen to each other more objectively.

• Helps the mediator organize the issues to determine the order in which they should be discussed. Usually the mediator will wish to focus first on the issues that appear to be the easiest to resolve. If students agree on some things quickly, they will develop a momentum for resolving all their issues.

• Slows down the interaction between the students and therefore allows a continual cooling-off process.

Exchanging Reasons for Positions

After disputants clearly communicate their wants and feelings, they are ready to exchange the reasons for their positions. In this part of the mediation process, the mediator helps students present their reasons, separate interests from positions, reframe the issue, and stay focused. Other responsibilities include ensuring that power is equal and recognizing constructive behaviors.

Presenting Reasons

Many people are not aware of what their interests are or why they are engaging in a conflict. They are so focused on what they want that they have not thought about their reasons for wanting what they do. The mediator helps students clarify their reasons for engaging in the conflict and thus to understand what is motivating them. Disputants can then negotiate an agreement to resolve their real problem.

When sharing their reasons, students must try not to confuse each other or sabotage opportunities to reach an agreement later. Presenting reasons in a way that promotes open-minded consideration rather than closed-minded defensiveness is a skill that often requires the mediator's help.

Separating Interests from Positions

By defining each person's interest and position, the mediator clearly separates the two concerns. An example is the conflict between Meg and Jim, who both want the baseball. Meg wants the ball to practice catching. Jim wants the ball to practice throwing. Their positions—"I want the baseball"—are opposed, but their interests are not. Underlying interests often do not conflict and can lead to finding a solution that satisfies both people.

Reframing

Reframing means thinking of the conflict and the other person's actions from another angle. Mediators can use several methods to help students reframe their perceptions:

- Viewing the conflict as a mutual problem to be jointly solved rather than as a win-lose situation.
- Changing perspectives.
- Distinguishing between the intent of an action and the actual result of the action.
- Continuing to differentiate between disputants' interests and reasoning. Seeking additional information about the other person's reasoning will result in a new "frame" emerging.
- Exploring the multiple meanings of any one behavior. When students seem stuck, the mediator asks, "What else might that behavior mean?" The more different answers a student can think of, the more likely the student can perceive a way to resolve the conflict. When students complain about each other's behavior, for example, "He's too mean," "She's too picky," the mediator should say, "Think of situations in which that same behavior would be positive." A positive context changes the behavior's meaning.

Staying Focused

The mediator helps disputants avoid tangents by keeping them focused on the problem, not on their anger toward each other. A common situation occurs when one person makes an angry remark, the other person objects, and soon the two are fighting over each other's insults rather than over the issue that began the conflict in the first place. For example, a student may say, "Did you hear what he said? He always tries to hurt me!" Such statements change the topic of conversation to the tangent of whether the remark was really meant to hurt or not. The mediator needs to redirect the disputants' energies toward solving the problem.

Equalizing Power

It is hard for a low-power person to negotiate with a high-power person and vice versa. Meeting in a neutral place can help equalize power. Another equalizing tactic is the mediator's helping the less articulate person state his or her wants, feelings, and reasons.

Recognizing Constructive Behaviors

The mediator should compliment students when they use negotiating skills, and shape their behavior by reinforcing "successive approximations" of skillful negotiating.

Reversing Perspectives

Mediators will need to insist many times that disputants understand each other's perspective. Reaching an agreement that is fair to both sides requires such repetition. One person may not understand why another person is upset, saying an issue that the other cares about is "no big deal."

Joan and Ron's problem is an example. Joan claims that Ron "bugs her" by calling her on the phone all the time. Joan and Ron have dated a few times, and Ron wants to go steady. Joan wants to date other boys. She is angry that Ron keeps calling her every night. Ron says, "What's the big deal. So I call her. That's no crime. She's just looking for a fight." Ron needs to put himself in Joan's shoes to see the conflict from her perspective and understand why she believes the problem is important.

Role reversal, or perspective reversal, is a dramatic way to solve stubborn conflicts. The mediator follows a general scenario, which can be used within the framework of two methods. The scenario follows:

1. Ask Student A to present Student B's wants, feelings, and reasoning.

2. Ask Student B whether Student A was accurate.

3. Ask Student B to present Student A's wants, feelings, and reasoning.

4. Ask Student A whether Student B was accurate.

Method One

1. Students change chairs or hats to symbolize the taking of each other's perspective.

2. Student A presents Student B's wants, feelings, and reasoning. Student B listens carefully, clarifies unclear areas, corrects errors, and adds omissions.

3. Student B presents Students A's wants, feelings, and reasoning. Student A listens carefully, clarifies unclear areas, corrects errors, and adds omissions.

4. Students change back to their original chair or hat and wait for the mediator to take them to the next step of negotiating.

Method Two

1. Students role-play the events leading to and causing their conflict. Other students may be brought in to role-play their parts in the conflict.

2. Freeze the role-play at the point after the conflict begins.

3. Students switch roles and continue, so that they are taking the other person's role and, in effect, arguing against themselves.

4. Stop the role-play after the players have gotten the feel of the other person's point of view. Discuss the role-play and see if any new alternative solutions have occurred to the students engaged in the conflict.

Creating Options

Mediators do not solve problems for other students. As student mediators have said, "The only right solution is your solution. We're not here to suggest the answer. We're here to listen. Check your ego at the door. You're in it for two people. You have to put your own feelings aside."

Mutual Benefits

The mediator asks Student A then Student B what they can do here and now to resolve the conflict: "We've talked about what's already happened. Where do we go from here?" Students should generate at least three acceptable, mutually beneficial options. The options should represent an ideal outcome that students can accept because it allows them to achieve their goals. Asking the following questions helps evaluate each alternative:

• "Is the option specific?" "Does it tell when, where, who, and how?"

• "Is the option realistic?" "Can students do what they say they will?"

• "Are responsibilities shared?" "Are both students agreeing to do something?" The mediator says, "Is this solution acceptable to you?" never, "That's a fair solution, isn't it?"

Sometimes students become fixated on one possible agreement and are unable to think of alternatives. Mediators can break this fixation.

Generating a series of options requires divergent thinking and creative problem solving. Mediators ask students to think divergently before they converge on an agreement. Mediators may also suggest possible alternative agreements that students have overlooked.

Students may be so focused on their disagreements that they are blind to the interests they share. Introducing a statement with, "I hear you both agreeing that" points out the overlap in interests and helps students recognize that they do share common ground.

Jose claims that Bobbie stole his lunch tickets. Bobbie denies it. There are no witnesses. So whom does the mediator believe? Often, the mediator will never know what really happened in the past. No one will ever know. So what can students do? How will Jose and Bobbie resolve their conflict if they disagree about what happened in the past? The answer is to focus on the future. Jose and Bobbie may never be able to agree on what happened to the lunch tickets, but they can agree that they are in crisis now. They can develop an agreement that will specify how they will relate in the future. A future-oriented agreement will not force anyone to admit wrongdoing. It will only specify what they are to do now.

Mediators can increase students' motivation to resolve the conflict by highlighting the gains for resolution and the costs for no resolution. In the example of Ron calling Joan too much, a benefit is that if Ron apologizes, Joan will date him. Some costs are that Joan will not date him and he will not be invited to her friends' parties, thus not seeing her very often. To bring about a resolution, the mediator may say, "Ron, what would you be willing to do to have Joan and her friends happy with you?"

Students can consider agreements based on package deals and trade-offs. Package deals resolve several issues at the same time. Trade-offs exchange two different things of comparable value. For example, what if Ron proposes a trade-off where he will not call Joan every night if she will date only him—would this be acceptable to Joan? The answer is no. Not dating anyone but Ron is "worth" much more than limiting the number of phone calls. Mediators help disputants make sure that the proposed items to be traded are of comparable value.

If students will not agree to resolve an issue, the mediator may be able to get them to agree to a principle. Two students may not agree on whether one should replace a lost book. But they may be willing to agree to the principle that it is wrong to solve problems by fighting. If they agree on that principle, then perhaps they can agree not to fight each other in future conflicts.

Conflicts may revolve around damages that require one disputant to make restitution to the other. Agreements may not be possible unless one student agrees to repair the damage caused by his or her actions. Restitution makes amends for injury, mistreatment, or insult. If a student breaks a window, restitution is made by paying for the cost of installing a new window. If a student borrows a classmate's book and loses it, restitution is made by replacing the book. When a person has been insulted, restitution may be made through an apology. Mediators assist students in agreeing on how restitution can be made.

Students can develop compromises that both can live with if time runs out. But keep in mind that compromises are inferior to integrative agreements. Compromises are often unstable because neither disputant gets all of what he or she wants, and the relationship is not fully repaired. The conflict, therefore, may reappear in the future.

If disputants cannot create possible integrative agreements, the mediator returns to considering disputants' goals and the reasons underlying the wants and feelings. Understanding disputants' interests is sometimes like peeling an onion. Disputants discuss one layer at a time, and the discussion reveals another layer underneath. Eventually, the interests are defined in a way that allows participants to identify integrative agreements. Questions such as "What did you do that made A so upset with you?" and "Why are you upset at A?" may help uncover those interests.

If disputants have difficulty in identifying their interests and potential agreements, the mediator may wish to have them role-play the events leading up to the conflict and the initial stages of the conflict. This procedure is one of the most helpful for encouraging students to think of optional agreements.

Balance Sheets

After students have identified at least three good agreements, they need to complete a balance sheet on each one to determine what the actual agreement will be. A balance sheet shows the gains and losses for each disputant and for interested third parties (such as mutual friends) if the agreement is adopted. The agreement that is most beneficial for both disputants is the best one. As part of the evaluation, the mediator asks disputants what they could do differently in the future if the same problem arises again. The more specific the answers, the better.

Reaching a Wise Agreement

The goal of mediation is to reach a wise agreement. A wise agreement is fair and based on principles, strengthens disputants' ability to work together cooperatively, and improves disputants' ability to resolve future conflicts constructively. The agreement should include the ways each disputant will act differently in the future and how the agreement will be reviewed and renegotiated if it turns out to be unworkable.

Mediators help disputants think realistically about possible solutions. For example, Davy and Terry got into a fight over which group would use the basketball court on the playground. Terry states, "The only sure way to avoid future fights is for Davy to transfer to another school." The mediator may wish to point out, perhaps in a humorous way, how unrealistic that proposed alternative is. Humor in the mediation process is a necessity. Laughter is the best cure for conflict.

If students cannot reach an agreement, the mediator has the last word—and it should be positive. Mediators tell disputants they appreciated that the disputants tried to reach an agreement; they are sorry disputants did not resolve the conflict; and they are hopeful that disputants will be able to resolve the conflict constructively in the future.

Formalize the Agreement

When an agreement is reached, the mediator completes a Mediation Report Form. The mediator makes sure all dates and names are correct and describes what disputants have agreed to do to resolve the conflict. Each issue requires a separate paragraph. The present tense is used. The agreement includes only the promises and commitments each person has made to the other. Each paragraph should begin, " _____ (person's name) agrees to _____ (terms of agreement)." The agreement does not include phrases that imply wrongdoing, such as "Ron agrees never to harass Sally again." If only part of the issues are resolved, the mediator may wish to list the issues that still need resolution.

Each student signs the agreement, and the mediator signs as a witness. Students and mediator receive a copy. Signing the Mediation Report Form formalizes the agreement between students and signifies that they will abide by it. The mediator congratulates them both, then in front of the students, rips up any notes that he or she has made. To prevent rumors, students should tell their friends that the conflict is ended. The mediator becomes the keeper of the contract and verifies that students are doing what they have agreed to do. If the agreement breaks down, the mediator reconvenes the mediation session and helps the disputants negotiate again.

Finally, the mediator congratulates himself or herself after the disputants leave. Mediators should take satisfaction from helping others: "We're all like hidden gold mines."

When the student mediator is unsuccessful in helping disputants resolve the conflict, it is referred to a teacher. The teacher then mediates the conflict, using the same procedures that the peer mediator used. If teacher mediation fails, the teacher arbitrates.

Preventing Future Conflicts

Students cannot always negotiate a resolution. When they repeatedly engage in destructively managed conflicts, and mediation and arbitration do not help, the mediator can take steps to prevent the occurrence of future conflicts. Such action requires understanding the circumstances that brought about the conflict:

• Barriers that prevent problem-solving negotiations (Walton 1987). Internal barriers include negative attitudes, values, fears, anxieties, and habitual patterns of avoiding conflict. External barriers include task requirements, group norms for avoiding conflict, pressure to maintain a congenial public image, and faulty perceptions of one's vulnerability and others' strength. Physical separation is a frequently used barrier to prevent disputants from expressing conflicts of interest. Examples are placing students in different locations, making sure they are not in the same room with certain other students, and removing a member from a group that is engaged in a conflict.

• Events that trigger the conflict (Walton 1987). A triggering event may be as simple as two group members who are physically near each other or as complex as two students in competition. Negative remarks, sarcasm, and criticism on sensitive points, as well as the feeling of being deprived, neglected, or ignored, are common triggering events.

• Entry state of disputants. A disputant's entry state is that person's ability to deal constructively with the conflict. A person's level of self-awareness, ability to control his or her behavior, interpersonal skills, and ability to cope with stress and adversity influence how well that person can handle a conflict. If a disputant is too angry, anxious, defensive, psychologically unstable, or stuck in the status quo to negotiate effectively, then negotiations should be delayed or avoided.

After analyzing the circumstances, the mediator chooses the time and place for negotiations. To avoid the conflict, the mediator removes the triggering events, builds up barriers to negotiations, and ignores the entry state of disputants. To initiate negotiations, the mediator increases the frequency of the triggering events, decreases the barriers to negotiations, and provides the support and help needed to ensure a constructive entry state for each disputant.

Tools for Negotiating and Mediating

The success of peer and teacher mediation depends on how well the teacher has trained students to negotiate and mediate. Tools can aid in the process. For younger students, the teacher may use storytelling and problem-puppet procedures; for older students, role-play.

Storytelling

1. Tell the story of the conflict situation using a "once upon a time" format.

2. When the story reaches the point of conflict, stop and ask the class for suggestions on how to resolve it. Make sure students give specific rather than general suggestions. Requiring specificity helps prevent a "give-the-teacher-what-she-wants-to-hear" response.

3. Incorporate one of the suggestions into the story, and then conclude the story.

4. Ask the disputants if this suggestion would meet their needs and if it is a solution they might try the next time they have a problem.

The following storytelling example is from a kindergarten class.

Teacher: Once upon a time, Jack and Jill were playing with a toy train. Jill was playing with the engine, and Jack decided he wanted it. Jill refused to give it to him, so Jack yelled at her and gave her a push. She pushed him back. What could they do?

Susan: Say they were sorry?

Teacher: That does not solve the problem with the engine. They both want to play with the engine.

Tim: You could take the engine away from both of them.

Teacher: The teacher is too busy. They have to solve this problem by themselves.

Ann: They each could try to grab the train cars.

Teacher: They tried that. It didn't work.

John: Why don't they share and play with the engine together?

Teacher: Actually, that is just what they did. Jill asked Jack if they could play with the engine together. Jack said yes, and they both pushed the engine together. Do you think that would work with the real Jack and Jill?

Susan, Tim, Ann, John: Yes.

Teacher: Well, from that day on they played happily ever after.

Problem Puppets

Margaret and Sarah are arguing over a set of blocks. Each believes that it is her turn to get the blocks. The teacher intervenes, calls the class together, and shows students two puppets. "These are the problem puppets, and they will help us solve the problem Margaret and Sarah are having," the teacher says.

1. Use the puppets to reenact the conflict.

2. Freeze the puppet role-play at a critical point in the conflict. Ask the class for suggestions on ways to resolve the conflict. Incorporate one suggestion, and finish the puppet play.

3. Repeat the puppet role-play until students have offered several different suggestions. Discuss whether each one will work to help children learn to think through the consequences of their suggestions.

4. Ask the children to pick the suggestion they think will work best. Retire the puppets.

Role-Play

Role-play can simulate real-life situations, making it possible for students to try new ways of managing conflicts without suffering serious consequences if the methods fail. This tool allows students to experience a conflict, identify effective and ineffective behavior, gain insight into their behavior in conflict situations, and practice the procedures and skills required to manage the conflict. Role-play is especially useful in teaching students to think metacognitively about the conflicts they are involved in. Sometimes they cannot "unlock" from their perspective enough to see the conflict from all points of view or generate acceptable, integrative agreements.

Students set up an imaginary situation in which they act and react based on assumptions and beliefs they adopt and characters they play. The role-play situation is not rehearsed, and the outcome is not predetermined. After initial instructions from the teacher, the actors decide what happens.

Before using the procedure with real conflicts, students should practice it in hypothetical situations. Teachers need to be sensitive to the fact that not all students like to participate in role-play.

Teacher Instructions

1. Describe the conflict situation, giving time, place, background, and any other information that will help students "get in role." Define the roles, ask students involved in the conflict to play the roles, or use volunteers. Help students get into their roles by introducing the situation in a way that involves the players emotionally.

2. Ask the players to act out the conflict. If they do not know what to say or do, asking them leading questions may help them get unstuck. Keep the role-play short.

3. Freeze the role-play at critical points in the conflict. Ask the class for suggestions about what can be done next. The players then incorporate one suggestion into the situation and finish the role-play.

4. Discuss the role-play by asking questions:

- "How could the conflict have been prevented?"
- "How did the characters feel in the situation?"
- "Was it a satisfactory solution?"
- "What other solutions might have worked?"

5. Make sure students "de-role" after the role-play has ended. Some students may have trouble getting into the role, and others may

have trouble getting out of the role. Announce clearly that the role-play is over and students should reflect on and analyze the role-play, not continue it.

A more sophisticated and powerful procedure is adding role reversal to the role-play. Role reversal is discussed earlier in this chapter in "Reversing Perspectives."

Student Instructions

When participating in a role-play exercise, remain yourself and act as you would in the situation described. You do not have to be a good actor to play a role. You only need to accept the initial assumptions, beliefs, background, or assigned behaviors and then let your feelings, attitudes, and behavior change as circumstances seem to require. The role-play instructions describe the point of departure and the beginning frame of reference. You and the situation then take over.

Your experiences in the role-play may lead you to change your attitudes and future behavior. You may have unexpected emotional experiences. The more real the role-play and the more effective the exercise, the more emotional involvement you will feel and the more you will learn.

Questions that are not answered in a briefing sheet may arise. Feel free to make up facts or experiences that accord with the circumstances. Do not make up experiences or facts that do not fit the role.

Once role-play begins, do not consult your role instructions. Be yourself after the action starts. Players should not act the way they think a person described in the instructions should act. Try to act as naturally as possible, given the initial instructions of the role.

9

When All Else Fails, Arbitrate

Ideally, students should be able to negotiate constructive resolutions to their conflicts. When they cannot, a peer mediator tries to help. When peer mediation fails, the teacher may try mediation. If teacher mediation fails, then the teacher arbitrates. If teacher arbitration does not end the conflict, then it is referred to an administrator. The administrator tries to mediate—if that fails, the administrator arbitrates. Arbitration is needed when the students are so hostile or have such opposed interests that they are incapable of reaching an agreement. The adults in the school have the final responsibility to resolve such conflicts; therefore, they need to arbitrate when negotiation and mediation have failed. It is important to remember that arbitration is the method of last resort.

Arbitration

Aesop tells of the bees, the wasps, and the hornet. A store of honey is found in a hollow tree, and the wasps declare positively that it belongs to them. The bees are just as sure that the treasure is theirs. The argument grows very heated, and it looks as if the conflict cannot be settled without a battle, when at last, with much good sense, the bees and wasps agree to let an arbitrator decide the matter. So they bring the conflict before the hornet, who is a judge in that part of the woods. Witnesses are called, and they testify that striped, yellow-and-black winged creatures (like bees) were near the tree. The wasps declare that the description fits them exactly. After some thought, the hornet states that if a decision is not made soon, the honey will not be fit for anything. He therefore instructs both the bees and the wasps to build a honeycomb. "Whoever makes the best honeycomb obviously is the owner of the honey," declares the hornet. The wasps protest loudly. The hornet quickly understands why—they cannot build a honeycomb and fill it with honey. "It is clear," says the hornet, "who can make the honeycomb and who cannot. The honey belongs to the bees."

Arbitration is a process in which a disinterested person makes a final judgment on how to resolve a conflict. Arbitration is voluntary when the people in a conflict request it. It is compulsory when a person such as a judge orders it. Within a classroom, voluntary arbitration occurs when students ask the teacher to decide how a conflict should be resolved after all other methods of conflict resolution have failed. Compulsory arbitration occurs when a conflict becomes so severe that the teacher has to step in to arbitrate it. Mediation is an extension of negotiation; thus, the mediator assists disputants in negotiating a constructive resolution. In contrast, in arbitration, an outside person makes a judgment; the arbitrator does not assist the disputants in improving their conflict skills. Disputants leave the decision to the arbitrator, who hears both sides and then makes a judgment.

Conventional arbitration consists of the following steps:

1. Both persons agree to abide by the arbitrator's decision. Agreement is based on the assumption that after disputants have presented their side of the conflict, the arbitrator will be able to make a fair decision. The arbitrator should be familiar with the subject matter of the case and have access to all available documents and evidence.

2. Both persons submit their desired goal to the arbitrator. Each party describes what he or she wants and would like to see happen. The arbitrator can then begin with an understanding of what the focus of the decision should be.

3. Each person defines the problem. Both have the opportunity to tell their side of the conflict.

4. Each person presents his or her case, with documented evidence to support it. No interruptions are allowed.

5. Each person has an opportunity to refute the other's contentions. After one person has presented his or her case, the other may attempt to refute that person's contentions. Both have a turn to show the arbitrator a different perspective on the issues.

6. The arbitrator makes a decision. After both persons have presented their case, refuted the other person's case, and given a closing statement, the arbitrator decides what to do. Usually, the decision is a win-lose situation—one side wins, the other loses. Winning or losing is assumed to be secondary to having had a fair opportunity to be heard. In essence, the disputants have had their day in court.

An alternative to conventional arbitration is final offer arbitration (Stevens 1966). Each disputant submits to the arbitrator his or her best, most conciliatory offer. The arbitrator then chooses one offer. Generally, research shows that final offer arbitration is superior to conventional arbitration (Bazerman and Neale 1982, Magenau 1983, Neale and Bazerman 1991, Notz and Stark 1978, Stark and Notz 1989, Subbarao 1978). Final offer arbitration produces more concession-making in negotiation and greater commitment to the outcome reached (Stark and Notz 1989).

Shortcomings

Arbitration tends to result in solutions that are less stable and less effective than those derived by negotiation and mediation. One reason is that disputants usually know their own interests better than a third party can. They are also more willing to commit to agreements they devise than to those a third party imposes. Arbitrators are more likely to dictate compromise solutions as opposed to integrative solutions that fulfill the goals of both parties. Anticipating that the arbitrator will split the difference, disputants may adopt a tough and extreme position, so that half-way between positions is more favorable to them (Feuille 1977; Magenau 1983; Stern, Rehmus, Lowenberg, Kasper, and Dennis 1975). Such an extreme approach is sometimes called the chilling effect.

Combining Teacher Mediation and Arbitration

Teachers and administrators usually engage in a combination of mediation and arbitration. Mediation is used first to try to reach an agreement. If mediation fails, then arbitration is imposed. This combination offers several advantages over mediation or arbitration alone:

• Disputants may be motivated to reach agreement during mediation because they are afraid that they will lose control over the final outcomes if mediation fails and the conflict is settled through arbitration (Pruitt, McGillicuddy, Welton, and Ury 1989).

• Students and teachers know that they will not have to deal with the same dispute again; a final settlement, whether negotiated or imposed, will be achieved (Pruitt, McGillicuddy, Welton, and Ury 1989).

• Another third party does not need to be informed of the dispute (Ury, Brett, and Goldberg 1988).

• A mediation/arbitration combination enhances the mediator's power, making disputants more attentive to the other person's recommendations (Pruitt, McGillicuddy, Welton, and Ury 1989).

Evidence that mediation/arbitration is more effective than mediation or arbitration alone exists (Kochan and Jick 1978; McGillicuddy, Welton, and Pruitt 1987). McGillicuddy, Welton, and Pruitt conducted a field experiment at a community mediation center. They assigned dispute cases to three conditions: mediation alone, mediation and arbitration by the same person, and mediation and arbitration by different persons. Mediation and arbitration by the same person produced the highest levels of problem solving; mediation and arbitration by different persons, the next highest levels; and mediation alone, the lowest.

Combining mediation and arbitration has two disadvantages. Disputants may believe they are being forced to reach an agreement under mediation because arbitration will result if they do not agree (Ury, Brett, and Goldberg 1988). The mediator may also become too forceful during the mediation session and shift prematurely to arbitration (Pruitt, McGillicuddy, Welton, and Ury 1989).

10

Implementing Conflict Resolution/Peer Mediation Training

Within the classroom, students traditionally bring their conflicts to the teacher and ask for assistance. Although teachers are responsible for ensuring that conflicts are managed constructively, they do not need to mediate each one personally. They do need to make sure that a competent mediator is available.

This book discusses teachers' primary responsibilities within the framework of implementing a conflict resolution program. These responsibilities are summarized below:

• Building a cooperative context where students resolve conflicts constructively. This responsibility involves using cooperative learning a majority of the time and carefully structuring cooperation within and among learning groups, so that the entire class is a learning community of collaborators (see Chapter 5).

• Teaching all students how to negotiate. Teaching the negotiation procedure and skills ensures that students are cooriented and use the same procedures for resolving conflicts of interests (see Chapter 7).

- Teaching all students how to mediate. Teaching the mediation procedure and skills ensures that students help each other become skillful negotiators (see Chapter 8). Because students know they will take turns as class mediators, they are more likely to be open to mediation and the mediator's suggestions.
- Knowing how to mediate if peer mediation fails.
- Knowing how to arbitrate if peer and teacher mediation fail (see Chapter 9).
- Implementing the peer mediation process.
- Structuring academic controversies so that students challenge each other's reasoning (see Chapter 11).

The Peacemaker Program

Once students learn how to negotiate and mediate, the teacher implements the Teaching Students to Be Peacemakers Program (D.W. Johnson and R. Johnson 1991). Students receive 20 hours of initial training in 30-minute lessons spread over several weeks. Teachers subsequently teach at least two 30-minute lessons weekly to refine and upgrade negotiation and mediation skills. The training focuses on what are and are not conflicts, how to negotiate integrated solutions to conflicts, and how to mediate peer conflicts. Two versions of the program are available: one for elementary and one for secondary schools. The elementary version follows:

- Each day, the teacher selects two class members to serve as official mediators. The teacher may choose students randomly or carefully match them. For example, introverted students may be paired with extroverts, or low-achieving students may be paired with high achievers. Initially, mediators work in pairs. When all students have enough experience to be comfortable with being a mediator, then they may mediate individually.
- The mediators wear official T-shirts, hats, or armbands so that students can easily recognize them. They patrol the playground and lunchroom. Generally, the mediators are available to mediate any conflicts that occur in the classroom or school.
- Conflicts that students cannot resolve themselves are referred to the class mediators. The mediators end hostilities, ensure disputants are committed to the mediation process, facilitate negotiations, and formalize the agreement.

• The role of class mediator is rotated throughout the class so that all students serve an equal amount of time. Mediating classmates' conflicts is perhaps the most effective and dramatic way of teaching students the need for using each step of the negotiation procedure skillfully.

• Teachers provide refresher lessons twice a week to refine students' negotiation and mediation skills.

The secondary-level program is similar to the elementary level, with two exceptions. School mediators are chosen from each grade level (two mediators for every 30 students), and the role of mediator is rotated throughout the school so that all students serve an equal amount of time.

Refining Negotiation and Mediation Skills

Gaining expertise in negotiation and mediation is a life-long process. Students, faculty, and staff need to overlearn the procedures by using them daily. Teachers should weave conflict resolution procedures and skills into the fabric of school life—teaching the procedures in classes, discussing them in the school newspaper, modeling them in faculty meetings, and posting the negotiation steps throughout the school. The norms, values, and culture of a school should promote and support negotiation and mediation procedures.

Follow-up lessons may consist of improving communication skills, ways to control anger, appropriate assertiveness, problem-solving skills, perspective-taking, creative thinking, and other related interpersonal and small-group skills (Johnson 1972/1993, 1978/1991; D.W. Johnson and F. Johnson 1975/1994). Additional work may also integrate negotiation and mediation procedures into academic lessons. Social studies, literature, and science lessons may be used to teach such skills. In an English literature class, for example, the teacher can give each student a novel and a mediation notebook. The notebook contains a schedule for reading and assignments, a section for taking notes on the reading, and a section on negotiation and mediation procedures. Working in cooperative groups, students engage in a series of instructional activities that teach them conflict resolution procedures within the context of the novel. Each major conflict among the novel's characters can be role-played and analyzed:

• Role-Play. The first role-play practices the negotiation procedure; the second, the mediation procedure.

• Analysis. Within a negotiation framework, students discuss what strategies the characters are using to manage the conflict and the resulting consequences of their actions. Within a mediation framework, students speculate on what would have happened if the characters had used the problem-solving negotiation procedure.

Since all drama is based on conflict, literary works contain many opportunities for practicing negotiation and mediation procedures in role-plays. The peacemaker procedures were used in a recent research study in a two-week high school English unit (Stevahn, Johnson, Johnson, Green, and Laginski, submitted for publication). Students were randomly assigned to experimental or control groups. The experimental group studied a novel, learned the negotiation procedures, and role-played each of the novel's major conflicts. The control group spent all their time studying the novel. On the last day of the instructional unit, students in both groups took an achievement test. Students in the experimental group scored significantly higher than those in the control group. The study showed that the peacemaker negotiation training, when integrated into instructional units, can increase academic achievement.

Conflict resolution/peer mediation training should be repeated yearly for 12 years, with an increasing level of complexity and sophistication. Students who have learned the training have a developmental advantage over those who have not. Trained students are more likely to gain career opportunities, obtain successful careers, build and maintain a lifelong set of friends and a cohesive and caring family, and generally enjoy a higher quality of life.

Research Support

The Teaching Students to Be Peacemakers Program is based on the theories of constructive conflict (Deutsch 1973), perspective reversal (Johnson 1971a), communication in conflict situations (Johnson 1974), and integrative bargaining (Pruitt 1981). The program has been implemented in schools throughout the United States and Canada and in countries in Europe, Central America, South America, the Middle East, and Asia. In tandem with this extensive implementation are research studies validating the program's effectiveness and theoretical underpinnings (Dudley, Johnson, and Johnson, submitted for publication; D.W. Johnson, Johnson, Mitchell, Cotten, Harris, and Louison, in press; D.W. Johnson, Johnson, and Dudley 1992; D.W. Johnson, Johnson, Dudley, and Acikgoz 1994; D.W. Johnson, Johnson, Dudley, Fredreickson, and Mitchell, submitted for publication; D.W. Johnson, Johnson, Dudley, and Magnuson, in press; D.W. Johnson, Johnson, Dudley, Ward, and Magnuson, in press; D.W. Johnson, Johnson, Cotten, Harris, and Louison, in press; Stevahn, Johnson, Johnson, Green, and Laginski, submitted for publication).

The studies were conducted in six schools in two countries from 1988 to 1995. The schools were in suburban and urban settings. Students in 1st through 9th grades participated. Most of the studies used control groups.

The findings indicate that schools are justified in their concern about the frequency and destructiveness of conflicts among students. Students are engaged in many conflicts a day. When trained, students successfully learn the conflict resolution procedures and maintain their knowledge throughout the school year. They apply the procedures not only in school settings but also in situations outside the school. When placed in a conflict where they can use either a win-lose or problem-solving approach, students tend to negotiate. The results also demonstrate that the peacemaker procedures can be integrated into academic units to increase academic achievement. Adults in the school perceive the peacemaker program as constructive and helpful.

Since little research demonstrating the effectiveness of conflict resolution and peer mediation training exists, these results are important and ground-breaking.

11

Using Academic Controversy to Enhance Learning

Have you learned lessons only of those who admired you, and were tender with you, and stood aside for you?

Have you not learned great lessons from those who braced themselves against you, and disputed the passage with you?

—Walt Whitman, 1860

Teachers can use conflict in academic lessons to promote motivation and higher-level reasoning, leading to higher achievement. Such activity also helps students experience positive outcomes from conflict, thus increasing a positive attitude toward it. Academic controversy exists when one student's ideas, information, conclusions, theories, and opinions are incompatible with those of another, and the two seek to reach an agreement (D.W. Johnson and R. Johnson 1979, 1989, 1992). Controversies are resolved by engaging in what

Aristotle called deliberate discourse—discussing the advantages and disadvantages of proposed actions. Such discussion is aimed at synthesizing novel solutions—creative problem solving.

A key to effectively using controversy to promote learning is combining social interdependence and intellectual conflict. The more cooperative elements and the fewer competitive elements there are, the more constructive the conflict will be (Deutsch 1973). Cooperative elements alone, however, do not ensure maximum productivity. Both cooperation and conflict need to be present. Thus, controversy is characterized by positive goal and resource interdependence as well as by conflict. In comparing four types of instructional methods—controversy, debate, concurrence-seeking, and individualistic—controversy is the only one that combines cooperation and conflict (see Figure 11.1).

Figure 11.1

Cooperative and Competitive Characteristics
of Instructional Methods

Characteristic	INSTRUCTIONAL METHOD			
	Controversy	Debate	Concurrence-Seeking	Individualistic
Positive goal interdependence	Yes	No	Yes	No
Resource interdependence	Yes	Yes	No	No
Negative goal interdependence	No	Yes	No	No
Conflict	Yes	Yes	No	No

What Controversy Looks Like in a Classroom

Using controversy for instructional purposes requires clear operational procedures (D.W. Johnson and R. Johnson 1992). An example of structured academic controversy can be seen in an English literature class where students are studying a unit on the issue of civil disobedience. They learn that in the U.S. civil rights movement, individuals broke the law to gain equal rights for minorities. During this and other difficult times, such as the antiwar movements, individuals have wrestled with the issue of breaking the law to redress a social injustice. In the past few years, however, prominent public figures from Wall Street to the White House have felt justified in breaking laws for personal or political gain.

To study the role of civil disobedience in a democracy, teachers place students in four-member cooperative learning groups. Each group is divided into two pairs. The teacher assigns one pair to prove how civil disobedience can be constructive in a democracy; the other, how civil disobedience can be destructive. To help challenge each others' reasoning and analyses, students draw from such sources as the *Declaration of Independence* by Thomas Jefferson; *Civil Disobedience* by Henry David Thoreau; *Speech at Cooper Union, New York,* by Abraham Lincoln; and *Letter from Birmingham Jail* by Martin Luther King Jr. The unit typically takes five one-hour class periods:

Class 1. Each pair develops its position and plans how to present the best case possible to the other pair. Near the end of the period, pairs are encouraged to compare notes with pairs from other groups who represent the same position.

Class 2. Each pair makes its presentation, with all members participating. The teacher encourages opposing pairs to take notes and listen carefully.

Class 3. Group members discuss the issue, following a set of rules that helps them criticize ideas, not people; differentiate between the two positions; and assess the evidence and logic supporting each position.

Class 4. The pairs first reverse perspectives and present each other's positions, then drop all advocacy and begin developing a group report that synthesizes the best evidence and reasoning from both sides.

Class 5. The groups finalize their reports and present their conclusions to the class, with all four members participating. The teacher evaluates the reports on writing quality, logical presentation of evidence, and oral presentation. Students each take an individual test and, if every group member achieves up to a predetermined criterion, they all receive bonus points. The groups process how well they worked together and how they can do better next time.

Theory of Controversy

Conflict is the gadfly of thought. It stirs us to observation and memory. It instigates invention. It shocks us out of sheep-like passivity, and sets us at noting and contriving . . . conflict is a "sine qua non" of reflection and ingenuity.

—John Dewey

The theoretical roots of controversy lie in cognitive development (Berlyne 1966, Kohlberg 1969, Piaget 1950), social psychological balance theories (Heider 1958), and conflict theories (Hammond 1965, Johnson 1966, D.W. Johnson and R. Johnson 1979, Maier 1970). All three perspectives posit that during cooperative efforts, participants engage in discussions in which cognitive conflicts occur and are resolved in ways that expose and modify inadequate reasoning, motivate new learning, and result in a reconceptualization of the conflict issue.

The controversy process consists of five steps (D.W. Johnson and R. Johnson 1979, 1989, 1992). First, students organize information and derive conclusions. When presented with a problem or decision, they arrange their knowledge and experiences within a conceptual framework, then use inductive and deductive logic to reach a conclusion. Preparing a position to be advocated clearly affects how well others understand that position and the level of reasoning used in thinking about the position (D.W. Johnson and R. Johnson 1989, Murray 1983). Students' conclusions, however, may be based on categorizing and organizing incomplete information, limited experiences, and a specific perspective.

Second, students present and advocate opposing positions. They follow a process of argument and counterargument aimed at persuading others to adopt, modify, or drop positions. When compared with students engaged in debate, concurrence-seeking, and individualistic efforts, those engaged in controversy contribute more information to the discussion; repeat information more frequently; share new information; expand on the material discussed; present more ideas and rationale; make more higher-level processing statements; comment more on their efforts to make high-quality decisions; make fewer intermediate-level cognitive processing statements; and make more statements about managing the group's work (D.W. Johnson and R. Johnson 1985; D.W. Johnson, Johnson, Pierson, and Lyons 1985; D.W. Johnson, Johnson, and Tiffany 1984; Lowry and Johnson 1981; Nijhof and Kommers 1982; Smith, Johnson, and Johnson 1981, 1984). The comparison also shows that group disagreements provide a greater amount of information and variety of facts as well as changes in the salience of known information (Anderson and Graesser 1976, Kaplan 1977, Kaplan and Miller 1977, Vinokur and Burnstein 1974).

The third step creates uncertainty, disequilibrium, and conceptual conflict. Group members advocate different alternatives, criticize and refute positions, and challenge each other's conclusions with information that is incompatible with those conclusions. Increased disagreement among group members results in more frequent disagreements, more people disagreeing with a person's position, and a more competitive context for the controversy. The more affronted a person feels, the greater the conceptual conflict and uncertainty the person experiences (Inagaki and Hatano 1968, 1977; Lowry and Johnson 1981; Tjosvold and Johnson 1977, 1978; Tjosvold, Johnson, and Fabrey 1980). Individuals are motivated to know others' positions and to understand and appreciate those positions (Tjosvold and Johnson 1977, 1978; Tjosvold, Johnson, and Fabrey 1980; Tjosvold, Johnson, and Lerner 1981). In addition, participants develop a more accurate understanding of other positions than do people involved in noncontroversial discussions, concurrence-seeking discussions, and individualistic efforts (Smith, Johnson, and Johnson 1981; Tjosvold and Johnson 1977, 1978; Tjosvold, Johnson, and Fabrey 1980).

In the fourth step, students search for additional information and view the issue from both perspectives simultaneously. When faced with intellectual opposition within a cooperative context, students search for more information, new experiences, and a more adequate cognitive perspective and reasoning process in hopes of resolving the uncertainty. Research shows that when compared with concurrence-seeking, debate, and individualistic efforts, controversy encourages more student activity in several areas:

• Searching for additional information (D.W. Johnson and R. Johnson 1985; D.W. Johnson, Johnson, and Tiffany 1984; R. Johnson, Brooker, Stutzman, Hultman, and Johnson 1985; Lowry and Johnson 1981; Smith, Johnson, and Johnson 1981).

• Seeking to understand opposing positions and rationales (Smith, Johnson, and Johnson 1981; Tjosvold and Johnson 1977, 1978; Tjosvold, Johnson, and Fabrey 1980; Tjosvold, Johnson, and Lerner 1981).

• Attempting to view the situation from opposing perspectives (D.W. Johnson, Johnson, Pierson, and Lyons 1985; Smith, Johnson, and Johnson 1981; Tjosvold and Johnson 1977, 1978; Tjosvold, Johnson, and Fabrey 1980).

Finally, students create a synthesis that integrates both perspectives. By adapting their cognitive perspective and reasoning through understanding and accommodating others' perspective and reasoning, students derive a new, reconceptualized, and reorganized conclusion. Participation in a controversy, compared with participating in noncontroversial discussions, concurrence-seeking discussions, and individualistic efforts, results in higher-quality and more creative solutions and decisions (Hall and Williams 1966, 1970; Hoffman, Harburg, and Maier 1962; Hoffman and Maier 1961; Maier and Hoffman 1964; Maier and Solem 1952); greater incorporation of opponents' arguments and information (D.W. Johnson and R. Johnson 1985; D.W. Johnson, Johnson, and Tiffany 1984; Tjosvold, Johnson, and Lerner 1981); and greater attitude change (D.W. Johnson and R. Johnson 1985; R. Johnson, Brooker, Stutzman, Hultman, and Johnson 1985).

How Students Benefit

Over the past 20 years, we and some of our colleagues have developed a theory of controversy, tested it in more than 20 experimental and field studies, created a series of curriculum units on energy and environmental issues structured for academic controversies, and field-tested the units in schools and colleges throughout the United States, Canada, and other countries (Johnson 1966, 1970; D.W. Johnson and R. Johnson 1979, 1989, 1992).

In a meta-analysis of the available research on controversy and achievement, D.W. Johnson and R. Johnson (1989) found that controversy produced higher achievement and retention than did debate (effect-size = 0.77), individualistic learning (effect-size = 0.65), or concurrence-seeking (effect-size = 0.42). Students who participate in an academic controversy recall more correct information, can more easily transfer learning to new situations, use more complex and higher-level reasoning strategies in recalling and transferring information learned, and are better able to generalize the principles they learned to a wider variety of situations. Controversy tends to result in more creative insights into the issues discussed and more syntheses that combine both perspectives. Students are more involved in a task. Such involvement is reflected in an emotional commitment to solving the problem and students finding the task stimulating and enjoyable. Studies with both adults and children, furthermore, found significant gains in performance, even when one or both sides present erroneous information in a controversy (Ames and Murray 1982). Conflict qua conflict is cognitively motivating, and its resolution is likely to be in the direction of correct performance.

Compared to debate, concurrence-seeking, no controversy, and individualistic efforts, controversy is also found to promote greater liking, social support, and self-esteem among participants (D.W. Johnson and R. Johnson 1985; D.W. Johnson, Johnson, Pierson, and Lyons 1985; Lowry and Johnson 1981; Smith, Johnson, and Johnson 1981; Tjosvold and Johnson 1978; Tjosvold, Johnson, and Fabrey 1980).

Controversies are not always beneficial under all conditions. They must occur in a cooperative context. Communicating information, for example, is more complete, accurate, encouraged, and utilized in a cooperative context than in a competitive context (Johnson 1971a, 1974). Whereas controversy in a cooperative context promotes more open-minded listening to the opposing position, controversy within a competitive context promotes a closed-minded orientation. Individuals are unwilling to make concessions to the opponent's viewpoint and refuse to incorporate any of the opponent's views into their own position (Tjosvold 1982, Tjosvold and Johnson 1978, Van Blerkom and Tjosvold 1981). Students need academic, cognitive, and social skills to participate in the controversy procedure (D.W. Johnson and R. Johnson 1979, 1989, 1992). Figure 11.2 summarizes the research findings comparing the four instructional methods.

Academic controversy has great instructional promise for educators. The four essentials of theory (Johnson 1970), validating research, integration into instructional procedures, and ongoing teacher training are all present. Controversy builds on using cooperation to instruct and integrates the constructive management of conflict into students' daily learning experiences. As students gain expertise in resolving intellectual conflicts, the stage is set for learning how to manage conflicts of interests with classmates and staff.

Figure 11.2
Comparison of Instructional Methods

Controversy	Debate	Concurrence-Seeking	Individualistic
Categorizing and organizing information to derive conclusions	Categorizing and organizing information to derive conclusions	Categorizing and organizing information to derive conclusions	Categorizing and organizing information to derive conclusions
Presenting, advocating, and elaborating position and rationale	Presenting, advocating, and elaborating position and rationale	Actively presenting position	No oral statement of position
Being challenged by opposing views	Being challenged by opposing views	Quick compromise to one view	Presence of only one view
Conceptual conflict and uncertainty about the correctness of own views	Conceptual conflict and uncertainty about the correctness of own views	High certainty about the correctness of own views	High certainty about the correctness of own views
Epistemic curiosity and perspective-taking	Epistemic curiosity	No epistemic curiosity	No epistemic curiosity
Reconceptualization, synthesis, and integration	Close-minded adherence to own point of view	Close-minded adherence to own point of view	Close-minded adherence to own point of view
High achievement, positive relationships, and psychological health/social competences	Moderate achievement, relationships, and psychological health	Low achievement, relationships, and psychological health	Low achievement, relationships, and psychological health

* * *

The frequency of conflicts among students and the increasing severity of the violence that characterizes such conflicts make their management costly in terms of time, energy, and money. To make schools orderly and peaceful places where high-quality education can take place, conflicts must be managed constructively. The sequential process discussed in this book offers one approach. We hope you will be able to use the information to implement violence prevention and conflict resolution programs in your school.

References

Abt, V., and M. Seesholtz. (Summer 1994). "The Shameless World of Phil, Sally, and Oprah: Television Talk Shows and the Deconstructing of Society." *Journal of Popular Culture.*

Alberti, R. (1978). *Your Perfect Right: A Guide to Assertive Behavior.* 3rd ed. San Luis Obispo, Calif.: Impact Publishers.

Ames, G., and F. Murray. (1982). "When Two Wrongs Make a Right: Promoting Cognitive Change by Social Conflict." *Developmental Psychology* 18: 894–897.

Amsler, T., and G. Sadella. (1987). *The Community Board Program.* San Francisco: San Francisco Community Boards.

Anderson, N., and C. Graesser. (1976). "An Informative Integration Analysis of Attitude Change in Group Discussion." *Journal of Personality and Social Psychology* 34: 210–222.

Bazerman, M., and M. Neale. (1982). "Improving Negotiator Effectiveness Under Final Offer Arbitration: The Role of Selection and Training." *Journal of Applied Psychology* 67: 543–548.

Berlyne, D. (1966). "Notes on Intrinsic Motivation and Intrinsic Reward in Relation to Instruction." In *Learning About Learning,* edited by J. Bruner. Washington, D.C.: U.S. Department of Health, Education, and Welfare, Office of Education.

Berscheid, E. (1983). "Emotion." In *Close Relationships,* edited by H. Kelley, E. Berscheid, A. Christensen et al. New York: W.H. Freeman.

Brehm, J. (1966). *A Theory of Psychological Reactance.* New York: Academic Press.

Burke, R. (1969). "Methods of Resolving Interpersonal Conflict." *Personnel Administration,* 48–55.

Burke, R. (1970). "Methods of Resolving Superior-Subordinate Conflict: The Constructive Use of Subordinate Differences and Disagreements." *Organizational Behavior and Human Performance* 5: 393–411.

Clark, M., and J. Mills. (1979). "Interpersonal Attraction in Exchange and Communal Relationships." *Journal of Personality and Social Psychology* 37: 12–24.

Cooper, J., and R. Fazio. (1979). "The Formation and Persistence of Attitudes That Support Intergroup Conflict." In *The Social Psychology of Intergroup Relations,* edited by W. Austin and S. Worchel. Monterey, Calif.: Brooks/Cole.

DeCecco, J., and A. Richards. (1974). *Growing Pains: Uses of School Conflict.* New York: Aberdeen Press.

Deutsch, M. (1962). "Cooperation and Trust: Some Theoretical Notes." In *Nebraska Symposium on Motivation,* edited by M. Jones. Lincoln: University of Nebraska Press.

Deutsch, M. (1973). *The Resolution of Conflict.* New Haven, Conn.: Yale University Press.

Dudley, B., D.W. Johnson, and R. Johnson. (submitted for publication). *The Impact of Conflict Resolution Training in a Middle School on Students' Ability to Engage in Integrative Negotiations.* Minneapolis: University of Minnesota, Cooperative Learning Center.

Feuille, P. (1977). "Final Offer Arbitration and Negotiating Incentives." *Arbitration Journal* 32: 203–220.

Fisher, R., and W. Ury. (1981). *Getting to Yes.* New York: Penguin.

Follet, M. (1973). "Constructive Conflict." In *Dynamic Administration: The Collected Papers of Mary Parker Follet,* edited by E. Fox and L. Urwick. London: Pitman.

Garofalo, J., L. Siegel, and J. Laub. (1987). "School-Related Victimizations Among Adolescents: An Analysis of National Crime Survey (NCS) Narratives." *Journal of Quantitative Criminology* 3: 321–338.

Hall, J., and M. Williams. (1966). "A Comparison of Decision-Making Performance in Established and Ad Hoc Groups." *Journal of Personality and Social Psychology* 3: 214–222.

Hall, J., and M. Williams. (1970). "Group Dynamics Training and Improved Decision Making." *Journal of Applied Behavioral Science* 6: 39–68.

Hamburger, T. (December 17, 1993). "School Violence Common, Data Say." *Minneapolis Star and Tribune.*

Hammond, K. (1965). "New Directions in Research on Conflict Resolution." *Journal of Social Issues* 11: 44–66.

Hartup, W. (1976). "Peer Interaction and the Behavioral Development of the Individual Child." In *Psychopathology and Child Development: Research and Treatment,* edited by E. Schopler and R. Reichler. New York: Plenum Press.

Heider, F. (1958). *The Psychology of Interpersonal Relations.* New York: Wiley.

Hoffman, L., E. Harburg, and N. Maier. (1962). "Differences and Disagreements as Factors in Creative Problem Solving." *Journal of Abnormal and Social Psychology* 64: 206–214.

Hoffman, L., and N. Maier. (1961). "Sex Differences, Sex Composition, and Group Problem Solving." *Journal of Abnormal and Social Psychology* 63: 453–456.

Inagaki, K., and G. Hatano. (1968). "Motivational Influences on Epistemic Observation." *Japanese Journal of Educational Psychology* 16: 221–228.

Inagaki, K., and G. Hatano. (1977). "Application of Cognitive Motivation and Its Effects on Epistemic Observation." *American Educational Research Journal* 14: 485–491.

Janz, T., and D. Tjosvold. (1985). "Costing Effective vs. Ineffective Work Relationships." *Canadian Journal of Administrative Sciences* 2: 43–51.

Johnson, D.W. (1966). "The Use of Role Reversal in Intergroup Competition." *Dissertation Abstracts* 27(9-A): 3121.

Johnson, D.W. (1970). *The Social Psychology of Education.* New York: Holt, Rinehart, and Winston.

Johnson, D.W. (1971a). "Role Reversal: A Summary and Review of the Research." *International Journal of Group Tensions* 1: 318–334.

Johnson, D.W. (1971b). "Students Against the School Establishment: Crisis Intervention in School Conflicts and Organizational Change." *Journal of School Psychology* 9: 84–92.

Johnson, D.W. (1972/1993). *Reaching Out: Interpersonal Effectiveness and Self-Actualization.* 5th ed. Boston: Allyn and Bacon.

Johnson, D.W. (1974). "Communication and the Inducement of Cooperative Behavior in Conflicts: A Critical Review." *Speech Monographs* 41: 64–78.

Johnson, D.W. (1978/1991). *Human Relations and Your Career.* 3rd ed. Englewood Cliffs, N.J.: Prentice-Hall.

Johnson, D.W. (1981). "Student-Student Interaction: The Neglected Variable in Education." *Educational Researcher* 10: 5–10.

Johnson, D.W., and F. Johnson. (1975/1994). *Joining Together: Group Theory and Group Skills.* 5th ed. Boston: Allyn and Bacon.

Johnson, D.W., F. Johnson, and R. Johnson. (1976). "Promoting Constructive Conflict in the Classroom." *Notre Dame Journal of Education* 7: 163–168.

Johnson, D.W., and R. Johnson. (1979). "Conflict in the Classroom: Controversy and Learning." *Review of Educational Research* 49: 51–61.

Johnson, D.W., and R. Johnson. (1985). "Classroom Conflict: Controversy vs. Debate in Learning Groups." *American Educational Research Journal* 22: 237–256.

Johnson, D.W., and R. Johnson. (1989). *Cooperation and Competition: Theory and Research.* Edina, Minn.: Interaction Book Company.

Johnson, D.W., and R. Johnson. (1991). *Teaching Students to Be Peacemakers.* Edina, Minn.: Interaction Book Company.

Johnson, D.W., and R. Johnson. (1992). *Creative Controversy: Intellectual Challenge in the Classroom.* Edina, Minn.: Interaction Book Company.

Johnson, D.W., and R. Johnson. (1994). *Leading the Cooperative School.* 2nd ed. Edina, Minn.: Interaction Book Company.

Johnson, D.W., and R. Johnson. (submitted for publication). "Teaching Students to Be Peacemakers: Results of Five Years of Research." Minneapolis: University of Minnesota, Cooperative Learning Center.

Johnson, D.W., R. Johnson, B. Cotten, D. Harris, and S. Louison. (in press). "Using Conflict Managers to Mediate Conflicts in an Elementary School." *Mediation Quarterly.*

Johnson, D.W., R. Johnson, and B. Dudley. (1992). "Effects of Peer Mediation Training on Elementary School Students." *Mediation Quarterly* 10: 89–99.

Johnson, D.W., R. Johnson, B. Dudley, and K. Acikgoz. (1994). "Effects of Conflict Resolution Training on Elementary School Students." *Journal of Social Psychology* 134(6): 803–817.

Johnson, D.W., R. Johnson, B. Dudley, J. Fredreickson, and J. Mitchell. (submitted for publication). "Training Middle School Students to Manage Conflict." Minneapolis: University of Minnesota, Cooperative Learning Center.

Johnson, D.W., R. Johnson, B. Dudley, and D. Magnuson. (in press). "Training Elementary School Students to Manage Conflict." *Journal of Social Psychology.*

Johnson, D.W., R. Johnson, B. Dudley, M. Ward, and D. Magnuson. (in press). "Impact of Peer Mediation Training on the Management of School and Home Conflicts." *American Educational Research Journal.*

Johnson, D.W., R. Johnson, and E. Holubec. (1992). *Advanced Cooperative Learning.* 2nd ed. Edina, Minn.: Interaction Book Company.

Johnson, D.W., R. Johnson, and E. Holubec. (1993). *Cooperation in the Classroom.* 6th ed. Edina, Minn.: Interaction Book Company.

Johnson, D.W., R. Johnson, and E. Holubec. (1994). *Cooperative Learning in the Classroom.* Alexandria, Va.: Association for Supervision and Curriculum Development.

Johnson, D.W., R. Johnson, J. Mitchell, B. Cotten, D. Harris, and S. Louison. (in press). "Conflict Managers in an Elementary School." *Journal of Research in Education.*

Johnson, D.W., R. Johnson, W. Pierson, and V. Lyons. (1985). "Controversy Versus Concurrence Seeking in Multigrade and Single-Grade Learning Groups." *Journal of Research in Science Teaching* 22: 835–848.

Johnson, D.W., R. Johnson, and K. Smith. (1991). *Active Learning: Cooperation in the College Classroom.* Edina, Minn.: Interaction Book Company.

Johnson, D.W., R. Johnson, and M. Tiffany. (1984). "Structuring Academic Conflicts Between Majority and Minority Students: Hindrance or Help to Integration." *Contemporary Educational Psychology* 9: 61–73.

Johnson, D.W., and S. Johnson. (1972). "The Effects of Attitude Similarity, Expectation of Goal Facilitation, and Actual Goal Facilitation on Interpersonal Attraction." *Journal of Experimental Social Psychology* 8: 197–206.

Johnson, D.W., K. McCarty, and T. Allen. (1976). "Congruent and Contradictory Verbal and Nonverbal Communications of Cooperativeness and Competitiveness in Negotiations." *Journal of Educational Psychology* 3: 275–292.

Johnson, R., C. Brooker, J. Stutzman, D. Hultman, and D.W. Johnson. (1985). "The Effects of Controversy, Concurrence Seeking, and Individualistic

Learning on Achievement and Attitude Change." *Journal of Research in Science Teaching* 22: 197–205.

Johnson, S., and D.W. Johnson. (1972). "The Effects of Others' Actions, Attitude Similarity, and Race on Attraction Towards Others." *Human Relations* 25: 121–130.

Jones, E., and K. Davis. (1965). "From Acts to Dispositions: The Attribution Process in Person Perception." In *Advances in Experimental Social Psychology,* edited by L. Berkowitz. Vol. 2. New York: Academic Press.

Kaplan, M. (1977). "Discussion Polarization Effects in a Modern Jury Decision Paradigm: Informational Influences." *Sociometry* 40: 462–471.

Kaplan, M., and C. Miller. (1977). "Judgments and Group Discussion: Effect of Presentation and Memory Factors on Polarization." *Sociometry* 40: 337–343.

Kelley, H., and A. Stahelski. (1970). "Social Interaction Basis of Cooperators and Competitors' Beliefs About Others." *Journal of Personality and Social Psychology* 16: 66–91.

Kochan, T., and T. Jick. (1978). "The Public Sector Mediation Process: A Theory and Empirical Examination." *Journal of Conflict Resolution* 22: 209–240.

Kohlberg, L. (1969). "Stage and Sequence: The Cognitive-Developmental Approach to Socialization." In *Handbook of Socialization Theory and Research,* edited by D.A. Goslin. Chicago: Rand-McNally.

Komorita, S. (1973). "Concession Making and Conflict Resolution." *Journal of Conflict Resolution* 17: 745–762.

Kramer, R., and M. Brewer. (1984). "Effects of Group Identity on Resource Use in a Simulated Commons Dilemma." *Journal of Personality and Social Psychology* 46: 1044–1057.

Kreidler, W. (1984). *Creative Conflict Resolution.* Glenwood, Ill.: Scott, Foresman.

Lawrence, P., and J. Lorsch. (1967). *Organization and Environment: Managing Differentiation and Integration.* Cambridge, Mass.: Division of Research, Graduate School of Business Administration, Harvard University.

Loomis, J. (1959). "Communication, the Development of Trust, and Cooperative Behavior." *Human Relations* 12: 305–315.

Lowry, N., and D.W. Johnson. (1981). "Effects of Controversy on Epistemic Curiosity, Achievement, and Attitudes." *Journal of Social Psychology* 115: 31–43.

Magenau, J. (1983). "The Impact of Alternative Impasse Procedures on Bargaining: A Laboratory Experiment." *Industrial and Labor Relations Review* 36: 361–377.

Maier, N. (1970). *Problem Solving and Creativity in Individuals and Group.* Belmont, Calif.: Brooks/Cole.

Maier, N., and L. Hoffman. (1964). "Financial Incentives and Group Decision in Motivating Change." *Journal of Social Psychology* 64: 369–378.

Maier, N., and A. Solem. (1952). "The Contributions of a Discussion Leader to the Quality of Group Thinking: The Effective Use of Minority Opinions." *Human Relations* 5: 277–288.

McCormick, M. (1988). "Evaluation of the Wakefield Pilot Peer-Mediation Program: Summary Report." In *Education and Mediation: Exploring the Alternatives,* edited by P. Kestner, V. Kim, and J. Devonshire. Washington, D.C.: The Standing Committee on Dispute Resolution, American Bar Association, Governmental Affairs and Public Services Group.

McGillicuddy, N., G. Welton, and D. Pruitt. (1987). "Third-Party Intervention: A Field Experiment Comparing Three Different Models." *Journal of Personality and Social Psychology* 53: 104–112.

Murray, F. (1983). "Cognitive Benefits of Teaching on the Teacher." Paper presented at American Educational Research Association Annual Meeting, Montreal, Quebec.

Neale, M., and M. Bazerman. (1991). *Negotiator Cognition and Rationality.* New York: Free Press.

Nijhof, W., and P. Kommers. (July 1982). "Analysis of Cooperation in Relation to Cognitive Controversy." Paper presented at Second International Conference on Cooperation in Education, Provo, Utah.

Notz, W., and F. Stark. (1978). "Final Offer vs. Conventional Arbitration as Modes of Conflict Management." *Administrative Science Quarterly* 23: 189–203.

Opotow, S. (1991). "Adolescent Peer Conflicts: Implications for Students and for Schools." *Education and Urban Society* 23, 4: 416–441.

Piaget, J. (1950). *The Psychology of Intelligence.* New York: Harcourt.

Posner, M. (1994). "Research Raises Troubling Questions About Violence Prevention Programs." *Harvard Education Letter* 10, 3: 1–4.

Prothrow-Stith, D., H. Spivak, and A. Hausman. (1987). "The Violence Prevention Project: A Public Health Approach." *Science, Technology, and Human Values* 12: 67–69.

Pruitt, D. (1981). *Negotiation Behavior.* New York: Academic Press.

Pruitt, D., N. McGillicuddy, G. Welton, and G. Ury. (1989). "Process of Mediation in Dispute Settlement Centers." In *Mediation Research,* edited by K. Kressel and D. Pruitt. San Francisco: Jossey-Bass.

Ray, Kestner, and A. Freedman. (1985). "Dispute Resolution Papers Series No. 3: Problem Solving Through Mediation." American Bar Association, Public Service Division, Special Committee on Dispute Resolution.

Rubin, J., D. Pruitt, and S. Kim. (1994). *Social Conflict.* New York: McGraw Hill.

Seligman, M. (1975). *Helplessness: On Depression, Development, and Death.* San Francisco: W.H. Freeman.

Smith, K., D.W. Johnson, and R. Johnson. (1981). "Can Conflict Be Constructive? Controversy Versus Concurrence Seeking in Learning Groups." *Journal of Educational Psychology* 73: 651–663.

Smith, K., D.W. Johnson, and R. Johnson. (1984). "Effects of Controversy on Learning in Cooperative Groups." *Journal of Social Psychology* 122: 199–209.

Stark, F., and W. Notz. (1989). "The Impact of Managerial Arbitration and Subunit Power on Bargainer Behavior and Commitment." In *Managing Conflict: An Interdisciplinary Approach,* edited by M. Rahim. New York: Praeger.

Stern, J., C. Rehmus, J. Lowenberg, H. Kasper, and B. Dennis. (1975). *Final Offer Arbitration.* Lexington, Mass.: Health.

Stevahn, L., D.W. Johnson, R. Johnson, K. Green, and A. Laginski. (submitted for publication). "Effects of Conflict Resolution Training Integrated into an English Unit on High School Students." Minneapolis: University of Minnesota, Cooperative Learning Center.

Stevens, C. (1966). "Is Compulsory Arbitration Compatible with Bargaining?" *Industrial Relations* 65: 38–52.

"Stop the Violence." (January 1994). *Scholastic Update,* 2–6.

Subbarao, A. (1978). "The Impact of Binding Arbitration." *Journal of Conflict Resolution* 22: 70–104.

Thomas, K. (1976). "Conflict and Conflict Management." In *Handbook of Industrial and Organizational Psychology,* edited by M. Dunnette. Chicago: Rand-McNally.

Tjosvold, D. (1977). "Commitment to Justice in Conflict Between Unequal Persons." *Journal of Applied Social Psychology* 7: 149–162.

Tjosvold, D. (1982). "Effects on Approach to Controversy on Superiors' Incorporation of Subordinates' Information in Decision Making." *Journal of Applied Psychology* 67: 189–193.

Tjosvold, D., and D. Johnson. (1977). "The Effects of Controversy on Cognitive Perspective-Taking." *Journal of Educational Psychology* 69: 679–685.

Tjosvold, D., and D. Johnson. (1978). "Controversy Within a Cooperative or Competitive Context and Cognitive Perspective-Taking." *Contemporary Educational Psychology* 3: 376–386.

Tjosvold, D., D.W. Johnson, and L. Fabrey. (1980). "The Effects of Controversy and Defensiveness on Cognitive Perspective-Taking." *Psychological Reports* 47: 1043–1053.

Tjosvold, D., D.W. Johnson, and J. Lerner. (1981). "Effects of Affirmation of One's Competence, Personal Acceptance, and Disconfirmation of One's Competence on Incorporation of Opposing Information on Problem-Solving Situations." *Journal of Social Psychology* 114: 103–110.

Tolan, P., and N. Guerra. (in press). "What Works in Reducing Adolescent Violence: An Empirical Review of the Field." Denver: Center for the Study of Prevention of Violence, University of Colorado.

Ury, W., J. Brett, and S. Goldberg. (1988). *Getting Disputes Resolved.* San Francisco: Jossey-Bass.

Van Blerkom, M., and D. Tjosvold. (1981). "The Effects of Social Context on Engaging in Controversy." *Journal of Psychology* 107: 141–145.

van de Vliert, E. (1990). "Positive Effects of Conflict: A Field Assessment." *The International Journal of Conflict Management* 1: 69–80.

van de Vliert, E., and H. Prein. (1989). "The Difference in the Meaning of Forcing in the Conflict Management of Actors and Observers." In *Managing Conflict: An Interdisciplinary Approach,* edited by M. Rahim. New York: Praeger.

Vinokur, A., and E. Burnstein. (1974). "Effects of Partially Shared Persuasive Arguments on Group-Induced Shifts." *Journal of Personality and Social Psychology* 29: 305–315.

Walton, R. (1987). *Managing Conflict: Interpersonal Dialogue and Third-Party Roles.* 2nd ed. Reading, Mass.: Addison-Wesley.

Webster, D. (1993). "The Unconvincing Case for School-Based Conflict Resolution Programs for Adolescents." *Health Affairs* 12, 4: 126–140.

Wilson-Brewer, R., S. Cohen, L. O'Donnell, and I. Goodman. (1991). *Violence Prevention for Young Adolescents: A Survey of the State of the Art.* (Eric Clearinghouse, ED356442, 800-443-3742).

Yamagishi, T. (1986). "The Provision of a Sanctioning System as a Public Good." *Journal of Personality and Social Psychology* 51: 110–116.

Yamagishi, T., and K. Sato. (1986). "Motivational Bases of the Public Goods Problem." *Journal of Personality and Social Psychology* 50: 67–73.